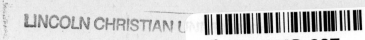

# THEIRS
## IS THE
# KINGDOM

# THEIRS
# IS THE
# KINGDOM

*Celebrating the Gospel
in Urban America*

ROBERT D. LUPTON

Edited by Barbara R. Thompson

HarperOne
*An Imprint of HarperCollinsPublishers*

HarperOne

All Scripture quotations are from the Holy Bible, New International Version, occasionally adapted by the author. Copyright © 1973, 1978, 1981 International Bible Society. Used by permission of Zondervan Bible Publishers.

HarperCollins books may be purchased for educational, business, or sales promotional use. For information, please e-mail the Special Markets Department at SPsales@harpercollins.com.

HarperCollins website: http://www.harpercollins.com

HarperCollins®, ▉®, and HarperOne™ are trademarks of HarperCollins Publishers.

Library of Congress Cataloging-in-Publication Data

Lupton, Robert D.
 Theirs is the kingdom : celebrating the Gospel in urban America /
Robert D. Lupton. — 1st ed.
  p. cm.
 ISBN 978-0-06-065307-1
 1. Church work with the poor—Georgia—Atlanta. 2. City clergy—
Georgia—Atlanta. 3. Lupton, Robert D. I. Title.
BV639.P6L87 1989
253'.09758'231—dc20         89-45252

14 15 RRD(C) 31 30

To Peggy, my wife and partner on this journey, whose compassion inspires me and whose integrity keeps me out of trouble.

# CONTENTS

# PREFACE

The year was 1971 and I was a young husband and father, just returned from the crossfire of Vietnam. I was convinced God had called me to minister to the poor in the inner city of Atlanta, but nothing in my semirural, midwestern background had prepared me for urban life.

My wife and I saw the city as a mission field and ourselves as missionaries carrying the light of the gospel into the darkness of the ghetto. How surprised we were when we discovered that the One who had called us already preceded us. Those to whom we came to share our faith frequently had more faith than we did. They had learned to depend on God for their daily bread, and answers to their prayers were often miraculous. Their capacity to care sacrificially for neighbors and family members made our scheduled, metered acts of service sometimes seem trite and even self-serving.

So it was that God's children who suffer most from crushing poverty became the very ones God used to speak to us of our own spiritual poverty. From those who had very few material possessions, we learned about our bondage to things. And from those who had much to fear and little to hope, we learned courage and faith.

The following reflections are glimpses into our eighteen-year journey on the streets of the city. Around every corner is the unexpected. Values collide. Beliefs are challenged. Emotions soar and fall. The city, I have concluded, is a dangerous place to walk, especially for those of us who carry valuable baggage. Much of what we hold dear is likely to be stripped away. But for every loss there is a gain; something of greater value is given. That is part of the wealth of the inner city, and that is why we have made the city our home.

Robert D. Lupton

# INTRODUCTION

"Look at them, walking down the middle of the road," we said. "Young toughs. They act like they own the street."

It looked like an act of defiance to my wife, Peggy, and me. It was one of those things newcomers notice immediately in a strange culture. We had moved into the city to work and make our home, and it was clear that overcoming our anxieties was our first challenge. We decided to take evening walks, a different direction each night, until we were familiar with our new surroundings.

Unexpected things happen when you walk down city sidewalks at night. Things for which one could hardly prepare. Things that the shadows conceal. Like a dog that lies in wait and then ferociously attacks the fence that only *he* knows separates you. And there are sections of sidewalk, broken and jutting, with which time and tree roots have had their way. They too lie in wait to trip the one whose mind is more on talking than walking.

Maybe the most unexpected thing of all was that we were not afraid. Not for the most part. Scary strangers soon became familiar faces. Staggering drunks became friends for whom we learned compassion. Young people, sometimes high on drugs, became individuals with names and families and special needs. Even those who were most elusive behind their locks and bars—the elderly—began to wave and respond to our "Good evening."

Of course there were the real and ever-present dangers. An occasional sociopath, the deeply troubled person who preyed on the unsuspecting and struck fear in the hearts of the entire community. Broken glass poised and ready to puncture the next thin-soled shoe to happen by. And tall weeds that reached out to scratch and cling. But for the most part we discovered that the real enemies of the street were alienation, misunderstanding, prejudice—those attitudes out of which most of our ill-founded fears sprouted.

More than seven years have passed since Peggy and I moved into the city. We still take our evening walks. It's our best time for talking and catching up on the busy activities of the day. It's a good time to confront the enemies of the street by remembering people's names and the little, important happenings of their lives.

And the unexpected dangers that lurk in the darkness? We've learned to elude most of them by walking in the street rather than the sidewalk.

Someday a newcomer to our neighborhood will remark, "Look at them, walking down the middle of the road. They act like they own the street!"

# THEIRS
## IS THE
# KINGDOM

## PART ONE

# Theirs Is the Kingdom

# MOTHER TERESA OF
# GRANT PARK

There is a saint who lives in our neighborhood. I call her the Mother Teresa of Grant Park. She has been an inner-city missionary for nearly thirty years. She has no program, no facility, and no staff. She lives in virtual poverty. Her house blends well with the poor who are her neighbors. There are box springs and mattresses on the porch and grass growing up around the old cars in her front yard.

She goes about feeding and clothing the poor with donations from concerned people. She works all hours of the day and night. She is difficult to reach by phone, and she doesn't give tax deductible receipts to her donors. To the consternation of her mission board, she seldom submits ministry reports (although for years she has faithfully saved all her receipts—in a large trash bag in her living room).

The Mother Teresa of Grant Park appears to have a poorly ordered life. She doesn't plan ahead much. She says she needs to stay free to respond to the impulse of God's Spirit. And that she does. Through her, God works quiet miracles day after day.

I, on the other hand, love order. I am of a people who love order. I was taught long ago to appreciate a neatly made bed and a well-trimmed yard. I am passing this value on to my children. We eat our meals together when everyone is seated and after the blessing is said. A calendar attached to our refrigerator door helps us organize our family activities. Order is a fundamental goal of our household.

Order is also a fundamental tool of achievers. It enables us to control our time, our money, our efficiency. We can arrange our thoughts, build computers, and soar to the moon. If a task of humanity is to "subdue the earth," then doubtless we achievers will provide the leadership. We are quite sure that God is a God of order. Our worship style and systematic theologies are clear reflections of that.

To the poor, order is a lesser value. Most pay little attention to being on time, budgeting money, or planning ahead. They may spend their last dollar on a Coke and a bag of chips to fill them up for three hours instead of buying rice or beans to last for three days. A mother may keep her children out of school to babysit so she can see the family's caseworker—trading the future for the present. A family seems not to mind tall grass, old tires, and Coke cans in the yard. Mealtime is whenever people get home. They seem to react rather than to prepare. Often their faith in God appears simple, emotional, even illogical. God helps you when you're in trouble and "whups" you when you're bad. He's good and does a lot of miracles.

Perhaps it cannot be otherwise when survival dominates a people's thinking. But something disquiets me when I reflect on these poor neighbors of mine and the Mother Teresa of Grant Park. Their "disorderly" lifestyles keep them from going anywhere, from achieving, from asserting control over their futures. Unless they change, they will never be upwardly mobile and self-sufficient. They will never be able to create successful organizations nor enjoy the finer things of life. They will remain dependent, simple, poor.

Now here's what bothers me. Why would Christ say, "Blessed are the *poor*, for *theirs* is the kingdom of God" (Luke 6:20)? Could it be that our achievement values differ from the values of his kingdom? And his comments about the first being last and the last being first in that kingdom—what does that say to us well-ordered leader types? You see why it disturbs me, don't you?

# WE BELONG TO EACH OTHER

Gray hair bushing out beneath her knit cap, she appeared to be in her late fifties. With one hand she tightly held a large purse that looked like a shopping bag; with the other she knocked persistently on the church door. She was visible through the security glass as the pastor and I walked down the hall, our early morning meeting on homelessness still fresh on our minds.

The pastor greeted her with as much compassion as possible for a busy urban leader running late for his next meeting. "Are you here for clo——?"

"No, no!" The woman interrupted him before he finished his sentence. Her countenance fell. "I'm here to help sort clothes." But the damage was already done. The spirit that moved this woman to spend her morning energy helping to clothe others was wounded. A simple error. Understandable. Unwitting. Irreversible.

"It is more blessed to give than to receive," said Jesus. But for this woman the blessedness of rising early to give to others was marred by her identification as a recipient. Her face reflected the hurt of lost self-esteem.

Receiving is a humbling matter. It implies neediness. It categorizes one as being worse off than the giver. Perhaps this is why we tend to reserve for ourselves the more blessed position.

In recent months I have been troubled by the lack of authentic reconciliation between the haves and the have-nots in our inner-city congregation. The woman in the knit cap may be showing me where our difficulty lies.

I came to the city to serve those in need. I have resources and abilities to clothe the ill-clad, feed the hungry, shelter the homeless. These are good works that our Lord requires of us. And there is blessedness in this kind of giving. But there is also power that allows me to retain control. My position as a helper protects me from the humiliation of appearing to need help. Even more sobering, I condemn those I help to the permanent role of recipient.

When my goal is to change people, I subtly communicate: Something is wrong with you; I am okay. You are ignorant; I am enlightened. You are wrong; I am right. If our relationship is defined as healer to patient, I must remain strong and you must remain sick for our interaction to continue. People don't go to doctors when they are well.

The process of "curing," then, cannot serve long as the basis for a relationship that is life producing for both parties. Small wonder that we who have come to the city to "save" the poor find it difficult to enter into true community with those we think needy.

"It takes everyone of us to make His body complete, for we each have a different work to do. So we belong to each other, and each needs all the others" (Romans 12:4,5).

I need the poor? For what? The question exposes my blindness. I see them as weak ones to be rescued, not as bearers of the treasures of the kingdom. The dominance of my giving overshadows and stifles the rich endowments the Creator has invested in those I consider destitute. I overlook what our Lord saw clearly when he proclaimed the poor to be especially blessed, because theirs is the kingdom of God (Luke 6:20). I selectively ignore the truth that monied, empowered, and learned ones enter his kingdom with enormous difficulty.

The community into which Christ invites us is one of interdependence. We are called to mutual sharing and the discovery of gifts Christ has concealed in the unlikeliest among us. And to those who consider themselves leaders, our Lord offers humility—the salvation of the proud that comes from learning to receive from the least, who are the greatest in the kingdom.

# PLEASE SIT IN MY CHAIR

She's sixty-six, mildly retarded, dangerously over-weight, twice a great-grandmother and a devoted member of our church. She lives with four generations of extended family in an overcrowded, dilapidated house, but her buoyant spirit is undaunted. Since losing her youngest son in a senseless mur-der last Christmas Eve (he was shot while riding with his uncle in a taxi cab), she has redirected much of her affection to me.

"You're my buddy," she says with a broad, snaggle-toothed grin. "I pray for you every day." Then she gives me a long bear hug. She wants to sit close beside me in every church service, and although the smell of stale sweat and excrement is often nauseating, she makes me feel a little special. Her internal plumbing doesn't work as well as it used to, and she leaves tobacco smears when she kisses my cheek. But I am pleased to have Mrs. Smith by my side.

She often hints, sometimes blatantly, that she would like to come home with us for a visit. Nothing would delight her more than to have Sunday dinner with my family.

But there is a conflict. It has to do with values that Peggy and I learned from childhood. We believe that good steward-ship means taking care of our belongings, treating them with respect, and getting long service from them. Our boys know that they are not to track in mud on the carpet or sit on the furniture with dirty clothes. To invite Mrs. Smith into our home means we will have filth and stench soil our couch. There will be stubborn offensive odors in our living room.

My greatest fear is that she will want to sit in my new corduroy recliner. I wouldn't want to be rude and cover it with plastic to protect it from urine stains. But I know it would never be the same again. Unknowingly, Mrs. Smith is forcing a conflict, a clashing of values, upon me.

Preserve and maintain. Conserve and protect. They are the words of an ethic that has served us well. Over time these values have subtly filtered into our theology. It is increasingly difficult to separate the values of capitalism from the values of the kingdom. Stewardship has become confused with insurance coverage, with certificates of deposit, and protective coverings for our stained glass. It is an offering, a tithe dropped into a plate to be used on ourselves and our buildings. Somewhere on the way to becoming rich we picked up the idea that preserving our property is preferable to expending it for people.

Why should it be so difficult to decide which is wiser: to open the church for the homeless to rest or to install an electronic alarm system to preserve its beauty?

Why should it be such a struggle to decide which is more godly: to welcome Mrs. Smith into my home and my corduroy recliner or to preserve the "homey aroma" of my sanctuary and get extra years of service from my furniture?

Is this not precisely the issue of serving mammon or God? How ingenious of our American version of Christianity to make them both one and the same.

We did finally invite Mrs. Smith to have Sunday dinner in our home. And she did just as I feared she would. She went straight for my corduroy recliner. And it never has been the same. In fact Mrs. Smith even joined a Bible study in our home the next week. Every Wednesday evening she headed right to my chair. She even referred to it as *her* chair!

I thank God for Mrs. Smith and the conflict she brings me. In her more clearly than in Sunday School lessons or sermons, I encounter the Christ of scripture saying, "Inasmuch as you have done it unto the least of these my brethren, you have done it unto me."

# THE IMAGE OF GOD

Behold an infant. A normal man-child in most respects. A kind-natured child. A child with promise and potential.

Watch him as he enters a rancid, smoke-filled world that resounds with the shouts and crashes of parents in conflict. Listen to him as he begins to compete for affection and food, and finds both forms of nourishment in short supply. His cries and soon his words become demanding. He pushes and grasps for strong boundaries that will assure him he is safe and loved, but finds only weak indulgence. No clear limits. No consistent discipline. Just impulsive beatings and permissive disinterest from parents preoccupied with their own survival. He begins to question his own worth. School confirms his suspicions. He drops out. He roams the streets at will, disguising his fear as nonchalance.

Behold a young man. A kind-natured, strong, undisciplined young man. Watch him as he falls in love, marries, and starts a family of his own. See his dreams begin to crumble as he loses one job, then another. He is evicted from a string of dingy apartments. His neighbors and "friends" spread rumors of child abuse and deprivation. The county takes four of his children. His wife loses respect for him. He is falsely accused of beastiality, arrested, and thrown in jail. Watch now as inmates and officials violate him. Watch as the last glimmer of dignity is choked out.

Behold a man. A broken man, scarcely forty. Parents dead. Rejected by his family. He walks the streets alone, head bent, shoulders stooped, hair matted, teeth rotting, drool running down his unshaven chin. A kind-natured man now babbling foolishly a salad of loosely connected thoughts and phrases.

"Worthless, but good-hearted," people say. Except when the volcano of hurt inside him erupts in rage. Then his eyes become wild. He claws and bats at his wife and remaining children. In time the wildness and heavy breathing subside, and he returns to his subhuman existence. He is prideless, worth less to his wife and children than the social worker that issues their food stamps.

Watch now as a miracle unfolds. A metamorphosis! The wind of the Spirit of God blows through and about Lester's life. A man made in the image of God and reduced to nearly animal form is slowly being restored. God begins to convince Lester that he has worth, that he is loved.

The message comes from many sources. A family who invites Lester and his family for a picnic. A businessman who continues to hire, fire, and rehire Lester on a job, insisting on a standard of responsible work yet holding on to Lester with firm love. People who notice and praise Lester when he is bathed, shaved, or wearing clean clothes. A person who accepts a gift from Lester without chiding him for "taking food out of his children's mouths." A minister who prays with Lester. A counselor who intervenes to cool flaring family tempers and helps Lester expose his festering hurt and anger to the sunlight of God's acceptance. The people of God, the Church, become actors in the unfolding drama of re-creation while the wind of the Spirit breathes in new life.

What potential is confined within this unattractive shell we know as Lester? Who knows save the Creator himself? But of this we are certain: when Lester prays or weeps with joy, when he caresses his baby boy, we see the image of God.

# FROM A BROKEN TREE

Ionce saw a large tree that had been struck by lightning many years before. The trunk was badly split and bent, but the growth of recent years was sturdy and straight. Bark had grown over much of the once-exposed heartwood, leaving the trunk misshapen but well protected. How is it, I wondered, that a tree could grow to strength and maturity around such a crippling injury?

I once knew a young man born in the inner city. His self-concept was badly scarred from parental neglect, racism, rejecting teachers, and years of failure. His values were deformed by the survival ethic of the street and by the hurt that had become a burning core of anger. I saw new growth form a protective covering over his open wounds and broken dreams. A strong new character developed, marked with unique sensitivities and perceptions. How is it, I wondered, that a young man can grow to strength and maturity around such deforming childhood experiences?

I once knew a Christian counselor whose life was marred by sin and whose character was bent toward deceitfulness. He struggled with rebellion against authority. His need for power was intertwined with his efforts to serve. He was plagued with insecurities. Spiritual and emotional growth, as well as years of socialization, largely concealed the kinks and twists at his core. But I knew how gnarled his character was, for I knew him better than anyone. How is it, I wondered, that God could use him to be a healer of others?

I have seen God take the broken, deformed things of this world, bless them with new life and sanctify them for his special purpose. From a broken tree, God provides shade in the summer. From a deeply scarred youth, he forms a person of unusual compassion and understanding, a model of hope to the disheartened of the inner city. From the twisted personality of a counselor, he shapes a healer of emotional pain and uses a rebellious nature for creative purposes.

I am reassured to know that the straightness of my grain is not a precondition of usefulness to God. And I am humbled to see that out of the twistedness of my wounds, he designs for me a special place of service.

## PART TWO

# When Winning Is Losing

# FOXES HAVE HOLES

I hit the button on my alarm at 6:00 a.m. The whistling at the windows told me it was another cold January day. I'd slept restlessly; the thermostat was slightly high and I'd fluctuated between being too warm with two blankets and too cold with only one. No matter now. The hot steamy shower woke me up, and my thoughts turned ahead to a day of meetings and projects.

At 6:29 I walked out the front door, bundled in scarf and coat against the chill, thinking of my first meeting. As I opened the car door, my heart froze. A man sat behind the wheel.

I reacted instantly, defensively. Not knowing whether the man was dead or dangerous, I drew my fist back to strike him before he recovered from his surprise. He slowly turned to meet my angry, startled face.

"What are you doing in my car?" I blurted out, my fist still clenched.

"I'm not in your car, sir," the man slurred in a frightened, thick-tongued voice. "I'm not in your car, sir," he muttered again and again as he slowly manuevered his body out of my car and teetered off across the front lawn.

My heart was still pounding as I drove past him on the street. It wasn't until I turned onto the expressway that my mind slowed down enough for me to reflect on what just had happened.

I remembered my thoughts in the shower about the thermostat. I had been glad our house was tight and well insulated.
There were worse things than sleeping too warm. I remembered also how good it felt to shave and slip into freshly
pressed clothes. And then I remembered how terribly frightened I was, how violated I felt that this stranger had intruded
where he had no right to be.

I began to wonder where the man was headed. His dark
silhouette stumbling down the street was vivid in my mind. I
hoped that his dull mind was directing him to his home. I tried
to avoid thoughts that he might have no home, that perhaps
the temporary lodging in my car was all the home he pos-
sessed.

Why? Why should it be, I wondered, that I am so concerned about sleeping too warm when another human being
equally loved by the Creator barely survives in a cold car outside my door? Why is it that I have a secure place to rest and
be restored, when this man, and so many others like him, has
no place to lay his head in peace?

The Christ, the despised one, the one from whom we hid
our faces, spoke softly, deeply in my spirit. It was the voice of
one who himself claimed to have no place to lay his head. I
began to weep. I remembered my clenched fist and my com-
passionless expulsion of this stranger from my life. I cried in
sorrow for a broken man whom I had sent off into the cold—
unshowered, unfed. And I sorrowed for one whose heart is not
yet sufficiently broken, whose heart hardens too quickly against
the call of the Lord among the least of these.

"I am sorry, Lord, for turning you out into the cold. Thank
you for using my car."

# ON THE CORNER

Watch them as congregate on the corner outside the liquor store. The rush-hour traffic drones by on the expressway overhead. Along the street merchants pull curtains of steel across their storefronts, snap heavy locks shut, and join others retreating to safer neighborhoods. But the streets are not empty. Small clusters of people, mostly men, are forming everywhere.

One by one they appear. They gather in parking lots, around fire barrels, in front of the billiard room, beside a late model Lincoln. A few are in cars; most are on foot. Some hold brown paper bags wrapped around pints of liquor or cans of beer. Others smoke reefer. A few have ingested or injected more exotic drugs. Ranging in age from fourteen to forty, they gather this autumn evening to tell stories, to boast, to "jon" [taunt], gamble, and establish or maintain their place in the pecking order of the street.

Move a little closer so you can overhear their conversation. A slim twenty-year-old brags about a sting operation that he and his partner pulled on a pusher. They made off with $600—"An' he can't even tell the man [police]!" Everyone laughs. A man in his mid-thirties with deep scars on his face tells stories from prison: the scams, the stealth, the con games he and others have gotten away with or been busted for. Younger eyes watch this veteran with the same sense of awe and envious respect that young men in older cultures reserved for the seasoned hunters of the tribe.

A young woman walks by. There are "oohs" and "ahs" and comments about her anatomy. A sixteen-year-old ventures an invitation to intimacy. She ignores him. The men laugh and taunt the youth about his ineptness with the ladies. Embarrassed, the boy defends himself with obscenities and swears that he has had countless sexual conquests. More teasing.

The conversation is now about women. A well-dressed man in his late twenties boasts of having five ladies in five separate housing projects. In exchange for his charm and manly prowess, they take care of his physical needs and pay for his new Old's Cutlass. The men around him try to top his story, describing ways they have exploited women for financial and physical gain.

Suddenly a young man erupts in violent threats and curses. He is angry at an older youth who has said something inflammatory about his mother. A knife flashes. A bottle breaks. Some of the men draw back. Others step in to separate the youths before blood is spilled. The older men know that this intentional provocation has nothing to do with the truth about one's mother; it is about proving one's order of rank on the street. The truce is only temporary. There will be another time and place to settle the issue.

Noticeably absent from the conversation this evening and every evening is talk of marriage and kids, of family plans and dreams for the future. Perhaps macho men don't talk of such things anywhere. But here, love is another word for weakness. It is something to be denied. Romantic words are merely tools for manipulating a lady's mind. Intimacy is a temporary high. Being cool, "fronting," "getting over" are the techniques for staying in control. These are being reinforced tonight, and every night, on the street.

You want to shout, "But this isn't real! It denies who you really are. Don't you have the same emotions, the same desires for deep and permanent relationships, the same hopes and dreams for a family as the rest of us?" But you remain silent, because you realize you have not yet seen life through their eyes. You don't know how it feels to be chronically jobless with no legal capacity to support a wife or family. You don't understand how strong young men get trapped in a permanent pool of unneeded labor at the bottom of our economic system. And you wonder: how does it feel to be both disdained by society and impotent to achieve within your culture even the most basic position of respect—the head of a household?

These men feel deeply. Their eyes tell you that. Their quick humor and creative use of language reveal the keenness of their minds. And now you begin to understand why they are here tonight: to belong.

On the corner no one asks them why they don't get a job. No one needs convincing about the dreadful reality of surplus labor. No women remind them of their inability to support their children or their inadequacies as husbands. Tonight women remain objects, so they can be controlled, dominated. There is no talk of commitment and security, of home and trust. There are no reminders of dreams that never will be.

Instead, they share adventures and intrigue, street success stories. Loud music, boisterous laughter, and other anesthetics dull their pain. It doesn't matter that they are outside the rules of societal approval. The unspoken agony of worthlessness is eased in the sharing of bottles and joints. Tonight there is relief from a future without hope.

# CHRISTMAS AGAIN

"Christmas again. Damn!" His words are barely audible but his wife knows his feelings well. She sees the hurt come into his eyes when the kids come home from school talking about what they want for Christmas. It is the same expression she sees on the faces of other unemployed fathers around the housing project.

She knows this year will be no different from the last. All her husband's hustle, his day-labor jobs, his pickup work will not be enough to put presents under a tree. They will do well to keep the heat on. His confident, promising deceptions allow the children the luxury of their dreams a while longer. She will cover for him again because she knows he is a good man. His lies are his wishes, his flawed attempts to let his children know what the older ones know but never admit: the gifts are not from Daddy.

He will not go with her to stand in the "free toy" lines with all the others. He cannot bring himself to do it. It is too stark a reminder of his own impotence. And if their home is blessed again this year with a visit from a Christian family bearing food and beautifully wrapped presents for the kids, he will stay in the bedroom until they are gone. He will leave the smiling and the graciousness to his wife. His joy for the children will be genuine. But so is the heavy ache in his stomach as his image of himself as a provider is dealt another blow.

Christmas. That wonderful, awful time when giving hearts glow warm and bright while fading embers of a poor man's pride are doused black.

# WHEN WINNING IS LOSING

I've always been competitive. Growing up I used enormous amounts of energy trying to beat my older brother at arm wrestling, chess, arguments, and anything else I thought I had a chance of winning. My competitiveness during these developmental years prepared me well for the business world I entered as an adult. The name of the game was winning, and I thrived on it.

My competitiveness reached its peak one day in my twenty-sixth year. I was flying door-gunner on a helicopter in Vietnam, and we were on a search-and-destroy mission. Suddenly the ground beneath us came alive with enemy fire. The intense battle that followed demanded the ultimate in combat strategy, skill, and commitment. The stakes were never higher and victory was never more exhilarating. I accepted with pride a medal for heroism in aerial combat.

It was only later, while still in Vietnam, that I began to understand the implications of my competitiveness. As I flew back from another "successful" mission, I realized that the emotions I experienced were the same I once felt while wrestling or debating. They were more intense because the stakes were higher, but they were unmistakably the same emotions. I was taking human life and feeling the thrill of victory. This thrill was inversely proportional to the agony of defeat—in this case death and maiming.

I began to suspect there was something wrong with a system in which my winning was built upon the defeat of another human being. When I returned to the United States I was unable to put this new insight behind me. I began working with disadvantaged people who were losers in a competitive economy. I saw young men, broken men, crippled by too many years of defeat. They could not find the inner strength to try competing again for jobs in the marketplace. I saw their children compete for education and job training, and weaken in the heat of the struggle because their bodies were poorly nourished and their spirits short on dreams. And although I felt unpatriotic for thinking such thoughts, I wondered if all was well with an economic system where winning meant defeating another human being. Could it be that among human beings cooperation was a better way than competition?

I pray that one day God will bring in a new order in which human beings will rejoice with those who rejoice and weep with those who weep. Perhaps on that day we will refuse the gains made at the expense of others and our success will be measured by the quality of our servanthood to humanity.

PART THREE

# A Little Leaven

# AND THE WHOLE LOAF RISES

Our greatest concern when we moved to the city was for our children. Any parent will understand this immediately. Peggy said it felt similar to the call God gave Abraham to offer up his son Isaac as a sacrifice—a terrible thing for a loving God to require of a parent. Yet at the deepest level we both knew God loved our boys more than we did and had their best interests at heart.

Our greatest challenge came the day we enrolled Jeffrey, age ten, and Jonathan, age six, in the local elementary school. Some of our friends urged us to put them in a Christian school to counteract the environment of the inner city. But we knew we were less likely to be involved in the public schools if our own children did not attend there. And the children of those we wanted to serve attended public schools. How could we authentically share the burdens of the poor if we allowed our privilege to insulate us from the hard parts?

So with much fear we walked with our boys down the street and turned up the steps of the worn old school building. We were greeted by the principal, smiling broadly, hand outstretched. He seemed ecstatic that another middle-class family was enrolling children in his school. When we asked if we could spend time in our boys' classrooms and bring other Christians to volunteer as well, he responded: "Do anything you want. Take the kids down to the church and tutor them if you like! We need all the help we can get."

In the next few years both of us, but especially Peggy, spent a great deal of time tutoring and assisting in the classrooms. A number of friends came from around the city to spend mornings and lunch hours with children who needed special attention. A school teacher volunteered to work with problem children and eventually joined our staff so she could commit herself full-time to working with nonreaders in the fourth and fifth grades. And she did bring the children down to the church to tutor them!

The following year several other parents with strong educational values enrolled their children in the school. The revived interest in the school was encouraging to teachers. With assistance from commited parents and volunteers, they began to make significant headway in the task of educating their students.

Gifts from concerned Christians enabled the teachers to start a summer tutoring and recreation program especially for children of low-income working parents. Children who usually slipped further behind each year and who otherwise would be left on the street all summer acquired a healthy headstart on the new school year.

Four years later, when the children of Slaton Elementary School took the California Achievement Test, a national standardized test, parents and teachers alike were overwhelmed at the result. The average test score was in the seventy-second percentile, an increase of more than forty percentage points! That meant the average child in this school, where most children came from poor, minority families, was receiving an education surpassing 71% of the school children in the rest of the country.

We were amazed at how little leaven it took to cause a whole loaf to rise. We were grateful to those who made themselves available to be used as good leaven. And we thanked God for quieting the anxiety of our hearts and providing quality nourishment for the minds and spirits of all the children in our community.

# AN INVITATION TO SUFFERING

I do not like pain. Not in any form. Loneliness, sickness (my own or another's), anxiety, frustration, disappointment, hurt—these are not the companions with which I choose to share my life. I actively avoid them. I buy drugs from my pharmacist to shield me from physical pain. I surround myself with people like myself who dispell my loneliness and reassure me that I am OK. I control my contacts with people who take more than they give. I schedule my days to eliminate disruptions and to accomplish the things I think significant or pleasurable. A theology of abundance, peace, and health has enormous appeal for me.

Recently I witnessed a small act in the drama of city life that both moved and troubled me deeply. It was a familiar situation. A family with three small children was evicted again for nonpayment of rent. Their ritual "put me up for just tonight" had been used once too often. With no money for bargaining, the only place they could find to stay was a front porch. The father slept under a bush. Although I was quite unwilling to give them any more, I wondered what would become of them.

Then an unbelievable but predictable event occurred. An unemployed brother whose own family was barely surviving took his evicted relatives in. Once again it was those who could least afford extra mouths to feed and were already crowded to the point of eviction who found it in their hearts to help. Even more disturbing to me was the cost of caring: increased hunger; hot, sleepless nights made even more unbearable by crying babies and wall-to-wall bodies; the stench of inadequate sanitation; short tempers; constant confusion.

This picture still burns in my mind. It is a haunting reminder of the energy I spend avoiding the cost of loving others. I establish an emergency relief fund instead of inviting hungry families to sit at my table. I develop a housing program to avoid the turmoil of displaced families living in my home. I create employment projects that distance me from the aggravation of working with undisciplined people. As a counselor I maintain some detachment with a fifty-minute hour and an emphasis on client self-responsibility. And even as I share the gospel with the needy, I secretly hope that God will handle their problems.

Of course I don't allow myself to think this way very often. I choose rather to concentrate on the positive things I am doing for people, helpful things, right things. But when I am honest with myself, I must admit that I cannot fully care for one who is suffering without entering into his pain. The sick must be touched if they are to be healed. The weak must be nourished, the wounded embraced. Care is the bigger part of cure.

Yet I fear contagion. I fear my life will get out of control, and I will be overwhelmed by the urgent affairs of others. I fear for my family. I resist the Christ who beckons his followers to lay down their lives for each other. His talk of a yoke, a cross, of bearing one another's burdens and giving one's self away is not attractive to me. The implications of entering this world of suffering as a "Christ-one," as yeast absorbed into the loaf of human need, are as terrifying as death itself. Yet this is the *only* way to life. The question is, will I choose life?

# SPEAKING THE TRUTH

There is a cancer quietly eating away at the lives of inner-city people. It is a more subtle disease than alcoholism, more hushed than venereal disease, less violent than rape but no less destructive. It seldom attracts media attention, but it is more pervasive than any disease on the epidemic list of the Center for Disease Control. This quiet killer is "the lie."

In the poverty culture of the inner city, the lie is a way of life. It is a tool the powerless use to get what they need (or want) from the powerful. It prevents courts from taking children, landlords from evicting families, caseworkers from cutting food stamps.

Perhaps the sickness would not be so severe if the poor used the lie only to manipulate and protect themselves from those outside their culture. But it does not stop there—the lie is highly contagious. Husbands and wives deceive each other with macho games and broken commitments. Mothers turn sons against absent fathers and manipulate them to become providers by whatever means the street affords.

Children, too, learn to lie to get what they want. By the time they are adolescents, the young men have learned how to deceive young women out of their virginity. Young women have learned to use their babies to manipulate young men. Both have learned to deny the truth of their own emotions. And when they have learned to live without trust or commitment, they are ready to face adulthood in a culture where only those strong enough to endure chronic paranoia and isolation survive.

Not long ago I was a member of a Bible study for young adults that met in a nearby public housing project. For a year we met weekly to read and discuss scripture, and share part of our lives together. Occasionally our prayer and sharing dipped below the surface into personal areas. But mostly we used cautious God-talk and politeness.

One week the dishonesty reached a level that disturbed the normally placid surface of our group. Richard, my co-leader, couldn't stand it any longer. "It's time to get real!" he declared.

In the following weeks that's exactly what we did. The surface boiled with deep emotions. Anger, distrust, jealousy, and fear mixed with tears and hollering and confessing and hugging. Admissions of illicit drug use and cheating on the housing authority came to light. Malicious gossip and slander were confronted. Anger at me for being "rich" and not helping more surfaced.

I was afraid the group would break apart under this intense pressure, but it did not. Instead its cohesiveness increased. Those on the fringes were drawn into the center. We sat for hours on cement floors and broken-down pieces of furniture, no one wanting to miss out on a moment. It was as if we had opened a gushing well of healing, life-giving waters in the middle of a parched, disease-ridden land.

Such simple truths—confessing faults to one another, speaking the truth in love, bearing one another's burdens. They are powerful medicine for those of us who suffer from the desperate disease of deceit. And strong medicine, too, for those of us whose deceit is neatly disguised behind spiritual facades.

# FAMILY VIOLENCE

Most serious physical violence in Atlanta and around our nation occurs in the home. It is between members of the same family, and it occurs in the evening. There is drinking involved and a weapon, usually a handgun, is used.

The violence evolves from heated arguments growing out of domestic turmoil. One half of these murders are divided evenly between husbands killing wives and wives killing husbands. The other half involves parents killing children, children killing parents, or relatives killing each other. These victims usually die in their own living rooms from gunshot wounds.

In an attempt to curb domestic violence, the Atlanta Police Department appealed to the Family Consultation Service (our counseling ministry) and numerous pastors of city churches to provide family counseling. I immediately brought their concern before a group of inner-city parents who served as part of our advisory committee.

Their response was unanimous: "We don't want family counseling!" I could hardly believe what I was hearing. With all the bloodshed and heartache, why would they refuse help?

As I listened, I began to understand. Most families in the city are poor. They depend on government aid for survival. Each of the various agencies to which they must go for assistance—food stamps, housing, welfare, health—has staff "counselors." For poor families, the counselor is the one who interrogates, investigates, and degrades them. Counseling is a necessary step to endure in the punitive process of obtaining aid. "They treat us like dirt" was the phrase I kept hearing.

"What we really need is a friend who is willing to help us with some of our problems," I heard. "Like unemployment, 'cause that's what we mostly fight about."

A friend, a person willing to be involved. Someone who cares more about them than about a program. That's what they were asking for. How sad that they should make a distinction between a counselor and a friend.

# THE APPEARANCE OF EVIL

Our 1977 Datsun was a faithful workhorse. But with 150,000 miles showing on the odometer and blue smoke billowing from the tailpipe, the time came for its honorable retirement. For several months, Peggy and I talked and prayed about its replacement.

At Christmas time a friend presented us with the keys to a late model shiny black Audi 5000 Turbo Diesel. We were speechless! It was an extraordinary automobile. One owner, well maintained, an ideal size for our family. Not even in our most aggressive dreaming and praying had we envisioned such a gift.

When we slipped into the leather seats and pulled out of the driveway for our first ride, it was sheer delight. The seats adjusted to our posture, the car handled easily, and a superb stereo system wrapped us in classical music. Perhaps it was our own enthrallment but people seemed to take more notice of us than when we drove our Datsun. Americans and Luptons love quality. What a wonderful gift from God.

A few days later, I gave a journalist a tour of our ministry. When we drove past our house he saw the Audi sitting in the driveway. I wished immediately it was parked behind the house, out of sight. I wondered what assumptions were silently forming in the writer's mind. What questions did the Audi raise about my integrity or that of our ministry? I wanted to explain that the car was an answer to prayer, not a symbol of self-indulgence. I wanted to say that it was not as new as it looked, that it was a gift. But since to explain would only make me appear defensive, I said nothing. I hoped he would conclude that the car belonged to someone else.

The car was a gift from God, wasn't it? An answer to our prayers? Why then did I feel uneasy about others seeing it? For years I had been bothered by the television evangelists who own gold Mercedes and Lear jets. And by the lady preacher of a poor church in our community who drives a new pink Cadillac Eldorado convertible that she says God gave her. Wasn't getting rich from ministry and lounging in self-indulgent comfort at the expense of others just plain sin?

But the Audi was different. It wasn't a Mercedes or a Cadillac. It was much further down the list of prestige automobiles. With no car payment, excellent gas mileage, and a long-life diesel engine, it was worth far more to drive than to trade. And trading down to a Chevy or Toyota would mean a loan. Debt was something we were trying to avoid. Good stewardship would lead us to keep the Audi and enjoy it as a blessing from God.

At a dinner table discussion, Jeff, our seventeen-year-old, commented that it seemed dishonest for us even to consider trading the Audi just to play into a "humble missionary" image. For all of our urban lifestyle adjustments, we were still rich by the standard of most of our neighbors. An Audi was an authentic expression of that reality. It was honest.

Peggy added that it didn't seem fair for our decisions to be controlled by the perceptions and expectations of people watching from a distance. We knew the Audi made good sense for us. Why should we let the uninformed judgments of others rob us of our enjoyment? The Audi was honest and it was right.

How strange it was that over the next few days I heard the voice of my dad replaying from the memories of my childhood. He had been gone for some years, yet his words returned with remarkable clarity: "Avoid the very appearance of evil."

His quote from scripture spoke of values of a different kind. The words called for sensitivity to the lifestyle struggles of others. They cautioned against wounding the conscience of a fragile believer or causing young faith to turn cynical. They spoke of Audis—the honest and right things in life that must be relinquished for the sake of others. The Audi was something good. But using money given for urban ministry among the poor to support the luxurious lifestyle of an urban worker, that was evil. Even its appearance was to be shunned.

So what was the higher value—good stewardship or avoiding the appearance of evil? What about the hypocrisy of driving a "humble" car when we could really afford better? Our motives are never pure anyway. Christians aren't supposed to judge each other, so why become captive to uninformed opinions?

I would have liked to continue this rational filibuster for the next several years while I enjoyed driving the Audi. But when I became quiet before God I was aware of that gentle nudging, familiar to all believers, toward the laying down of life and other valued things for the sake of brothers and sisters.

*Thank you, dear friend, for your generous and thoughtful gift. Although we could not keep the Audi, it brought us joy, struggle, and a deeper understanding of the life in Christ to which we all have been called.*

PART FOUR

# Who's Manipulating Whom?

# KURT

For a long time we sat on my front porch as Kurt unburdened his soul. I listened mostly. I couldn't comprehend that in thirty short years one person could experience so much pain. Kurt spoke about the horror of finding his mother's lifeless body, nude from the waist down and suspended between two utility poles. He told of the hate he felt for the men who molested her and then threw her off the roof of a tenement building. Rage had driven him for two years until he found one of the men responsible, but the torturous vengeance he extracted at gunpoint gave him no satisfaction.

In the years that followed Kurt suffered from alcoholism and drug abuse. There were months lost forever from his memory. He described the pain of having his face and jaw crushed with a baseball bat, and the constant fear of being found again by the men against whom he had turned state's evidence.

In spite of the brokenness of his life, Kurt seemed remarkably hopeful. He spoke happily of his marriage and his toddler son. He seemed motivated by his latest job and the better life it promised. Of course I would give him two dollars for his bus fare to and from work. It was only a small way of caring for a neighbor who had taken me into his confidence.

Alas, the two dollars never reached the coin drop on the bus. Kurt purchased a bottle and dropped out of sight. The familiar cycle of deceit, dependency, and failure began again. I had been used.

Kurt had been honest with me, at least in most respects. The story of his traumatized life was true. His emotions were and are real. There may even have been redemptive value in our long talk together. I hope there was. But when I realized that Kurt had a hidden story, one he carefully kept from me, I could not help feeling violated.

The affluent and the disinherited have frequent contact in the city. When impoverished people become desperate for food or a fix, satisfying that need becomes more important than anything. Pride diminishes and schemes emerge. The resources of others become their mark. Those who rob are perhaps the most desperate and daring, but those who manipulate are often the most skilled. The use of truth and half-truth, colorful descriptions, moist eyes, and urgent tones are powerful tools for eliciting compassion and dollars.

I tire of being hooked, deceived, taken from. But when I consider the safer ways of giving, the impersonal media appeals, the professional mailings that would free me from contagion and protect me from seeing the whole picture, I know I must continue touching and being touched. At least I am touched by persons with names and familiar faces. I can confront. I can express disappointment to the one who has betrayed my trust. I can be angry with or embrace the one who has taken from me.

And I can grow. I can see the conditions I place on my giving, my own subtle forms of manipulation. I am confronted with my pride that requires others to conform to my image. I see my need to control, to meter out love in exchange for the responses I desire.

I will opt to be manipulated in person. For somewhere concealed in these painful interactions are the keys to my own freedom.

# THE REFERRAL GAME

He was a bearded man. He was probably in his late thirties, although it was difficult to tell from his disheveled appearance. With the sleeve of his shirt, he wiped the sweat from his face and readied himself to make a proper reception desk presentation.

He was hungry, he told Trisha. Needed some food real bad. Trisha dutifully responded that our lunch was on Wednesday, but if he would go down the street to St. Anthony's. . . .

The bearded man cut Trisha short. He was no longer able to maintain a meek countenance. His anger flared as he recounted his last two days of trudging through the city, following one empty lead after another. He was now very hungry and desperate. He couldn't tolerate any more of this kind of help. He had come to the end of the Referral Game.

"Referral" is a game devised by people helpers to assist the needy in finding help *somewhere else*. It appears kind and is laced with compassionate words. It can be played by all kinds of churches and agencies. The only requirement is the purchase of a social service directory and a volunteer to dispense appropriate information.

"Referral" is an attractive game for churches. Christians can discharge their responsibility to the hungry, naked, and homeless with efficiency and cost effectiveness. Referral requires little personal contact with the poor. It can be done by phone. Serious players, of course, schedule five to fifteen minute personal interviews, fill out data forms, and even make phone calls on behalf of the interviewee. Some Referral fanatics have computerized the game, dramatically reducing processing time and adding a cross-check dimension that keeps the poor playing by the rules.

Referral, like Monopoly or Risk, involves true-to-life situations. It is often played with great emotion and intensity. We can learn a great deal about poverty, the system, and even ourselves by playing it. But for us Referral is different from real life. We can close the manual and go home whenever we decide.

Referral is a serious game. The pawns are human beings. *They* know what the players do not. They know there is not enough food in the game to feed everyone. They know the allocation of beds and jobs is half enough to go around. Yet the pawns continue to allow themselves to be moved from place to place. Perhaps they are hoping to find a Referral player who will remove his or her helper mask and become a real-life neighbor. More than anyone else, pawns understand that in *real life* there is an abundance of food and shelter. There is enough for everyone. And they know that real neighbors share. Therein lies their hope.

Referral is serious, too, because it deludes the resourced people of God into believing they have fed, clothed, and housed "the least of these." In fact they have neither shared their bread, nor given their second coat, nor invited a stranger into their home. Referral allows us to process poverty with rubber-gloved safety rather than enter the contaminating world of redemptive relationships.

"Damn racists!" the bearded man exclaimed with a glare. He turned and without looking back limped out the church door, slamming it behind him. A real person. Alone.

# ON FIXING PEOPLE

Most people saw Philip as a ne'er-do-well, a community write-off. He was an abusive father, a chronic manipulator, an irritating leech, and probably mentally retarded. I remember feeling relieved when he was locked up for a drunken escapade. At least he was out of the neighborhood for awhile.

That's how I felt before I glimpsed Philip through kingdom eyes. It happened one day while I was talking with our pastor. He had discovered some value in Philip that the rest of us missed. Apparently there was a rather keen mind behind Philip's dull appearance. And concealed by a host of irritating defenses was a heart longing to be tender and responsive.

At first I couldn't see it. But I wanted to believe it, so I made a commitment to invest myself in Philip. I convinced some people to create a job where he could learn the discipline of steady work. We secured affordable housing to give his family a stable living situation. There were hours and hours of counseling, teaching, modeling, and praying.

The changes that occurred were remarkable. Philip stopped drinking and assumed a leadership role in his home. His hard work began to pay off both in income and self-esteem. The church community became his family, and he demonstrated a genuine desire to grow as a man of faith.

By the end of two years, it was almost impossible to recognize the old Philip in the new. An incredible transformation had taken place. We all marveled at the life-changing work that had been done in him.

Then things started to unravel. Philip's work attendance became irregular. He lost one job, then another. As some of his old behavior patterns returned, his home life suffered. His participation in church declined. We talked, prayed, encouraged, and rebuked. Nothing worked. The backward drift continued and continues even as I write. We seem powerless to stop it and that troubles me deeply. Again and again I ask, "Why?"

Why, indeed? Perhaps it's time to look at myself. Does my disappointment spring from compassion and care for Philip? Or is it a reaction from a darker side of me that sees his downfall as the loss of my personal accomplishment? Have I watered and tilled and waited in wonderment for what the Creator would cause to grow? Or have I been clipping and twisting and wiring a miniature bonsai shaped after my image? Could it be that Philip shrivels because of the manipulation of my expectations?

I'm beginning to see that fixing people is a dangerous business. Fixing assumes I know what the final form should be, as if I were a spiritual orthodontist who knew just what wires need tightening to produce the perfect smile. When I presume to fix someone, I shape that person with my values, doctrine, hygiene, parenting, vocabulary, housekeeping, nutrition, and a host of other things. Fixing is a license to fashion after my image one who may be uniquely created to flower in quite a different form. It is a dangerous business because it may block or skew the growth of another. And it may unwittingly intrude on the work that God reserves for himself alone.

But what about Philip? How can I help him?

Or is Philip helping me? Perhaps he is teaching me to serve without controlling. The drama of his life instructs me in the ways of being a good neighbor. He invites me to take a faith-risk, to gamble that in releasing him from the shadows of my expectations he will be freed to grow toward the sunshine of the Creator. Do I really believe God is the designer of *all* life? Do I believe my highest and best is to love God and my neighbor? Is that what you ask of me, Philip?

# COMPASSION AND THE
# CLOTHES CLOSET

While remodeling our church, I came across a yellowed sign taped to the wall of an old storage room. Before tearing it down, I gave it a casual glance: CLOTHES CLOSET. But then I realized it was more than just a sign. It was a history. The lined-out, crayoned-in revisions and explanations told a fascinating story of the evolution of a ministry. Between the lines one could read of the classic struggle between Christians in charge and people in need. I gently peeled the document from the wall to preserve it for further study:

| *The sign:* | *Reading between the lines:* |
| --- | --- |
| THERE WILL BE A MINIMUM CHARGE OF 10¢ FOR EACH USE OF THE CLOTHES CLOSET. | A first attempt to control greed. |
| Up to 5 articles for 10¢<br>Up to 10 articles for 20¢<br>Up to 15 articles for 30¢ | The scratched out rules failed to limit grabbiness. |
| NO CREDIT | No money—no admission. Nice and clean. Testing credit-worthiness is too time-consuming, subjective, risky. |

COMPASSION AND THE CLOTHES CLOSET / 49

| | |
|---|---|
| No one can use the Clothes Closet without charge (unless they get a signed note from the pastors). | Revision of the no credit policy. An "appeals" procedure for those dissatisfied with stated rules. Legitimizes end-runs that are being made to the pastor. |
| No one can take more than 5 articles without a signed note verifying your need. | Definition of credit revision. Unless the pastor spells it out in writing, the five-garment limit prevails. No second party verbal interpretations. |
| The word "no one" shall be taken to mean either individuals or families. | Further definition of credit revision. Another loophole closed. The pastor's note could not be used as a free ticket by different members of the same family. |

NO SMOKING!

Can you envision the challenges, the rule tightening, the manipulative ploys and countermoves that took place between good church folks and the people they were trying to help? I smile when I remember how brow-furrowed we became about enforcing our one-sided legislation. Like temple police, we guarded the resources of the kingdom as if they were our own. Somewhere in the process the poor became our adversaries.

Anyone who has been given the unfortunate task of dispensing free (or nearly free) commodities can tell similar stories. Something seems to go wrong when a person with valued resources attempts to distribute them to others in need. The transactions, no matter how compassionate, go sour in the gut of both giver and receiver. A subtle, unintentional message slips through: "You have nothing of worth that I desire in return." The giver is protected by his or her one-up status. The recipient is exposed, vulnerable. It's little wonder that negative attitudes surface. It becomes hard to be a cheerful giver and even harder to be a cheerful recipient.

Ancient Hebrew wisdom describes four levels of charity. At the highest level, the giver provides a job for a person in need without that person knowing who provided it. At the next level, the giver provides work that the needy person knows the giver provided. The third level is an anonymous gift. At the lowest level of charity, which should be avoided whenever possible, the giver gives a gift to a poor person who has full knowledge of the donor's identity.

The deepest poverty is to have nothing of value to offer. Charity that fosters such poverty must be challenged. We know that work produces dignity while welfare depletes self-esteem. We know that reciprocity builds mutual respect while one-way giving brews contempt. Yet we continue to run clothes closets and free food pantries and give-away benevolence funds, and we wonder why the joy is missing.

Perhaps it is our time and place in history to reimplement the wisdom of the ages, to fashion contemporary models of thoughtful compassion. Our donated clothes could create stores and job training. Our benevolence dollars could develop economies within the economy: daycare centers, janitorial help, fix-the-widow's roof services, and other jobs that employ the jobless in esteem-building work.

"Your work is your calling," declared the reformer, Martin Luther. Does not the role of the church in our day include the enabling of the poor to find their calling?

PART FIVE

The Lord Loves a Cheerful Giver

# THE CHEERFUL GIVER

"I been straight for over a year now but I ain't sure if I can hold out much longer. A man can see his kids go hungry for just so long—then he's gotta do something somehow about it."

His voice trembled. Desperation showed in his eyes as he stared out my office window. No job, rent two months behind, friends all used up. Agencies unresponsive. His shoulders drooped. Tomorrow was too far away to think about. The children were hungry, very hungry. That must be taken care of now, somehow.

It was that *somehow* that bothered me most. It had a foreboding sound, as if something in him might be about to erupt. My immediate reaction was to prevent it, to save him from himself. Money for food would resolve the immediate crisis. He had assured me of this.

Why did I not feel compassion flowing toward this man? It seemed blocked by my fears of being used. I felt trapped. To question him would be embarrassing. Asking for validation of his story would insult an already hurting father. Buying food and taking it to his children myself would communicate my skepticism about him.

But to say "no" had the most serious implications. A "no" might be that last straw, the rejection that would push him over the brink. What made my entrapment even worse was that

I was a follower of Christ, wanting to serve those in need. The credibility of my witness was on the line.

I gave him the money. And I wondered as he thanked me graciously and walked away why I didn't feel any joy. There was only relief.

"The Lord loves a cheerful giver." To be a cheerful giver, one must be a free giver—free from coercion and manipulation, free from the emotional hooks that corner and obligate. Giving out of necessity to a good cause can leave a bad aftertaste in your mouth. But giving out of coercion to a need that is uncertain goes sour in your stomach.

When we first moved to the inner city, a thirty-year urban missionary gave me a nugget of wisdom. She advised me not to give an immediate response when people asked for help. Rather, I should listen carefully to each request, then explain to the person in need that I would spend time in prayer and get back to them. This was no spiritual-sounding put-off. It was a veteran missionary's secret to remaining a joyful giver. Pulling away from the emotional pressure of the moment enabled her to quiet her spirit, prayerfully assess her priorities, and determine in which needs to invest herself—responsibly, lovingly, freely. "Let each one do as he has purposed in his heart; not grudgingly or under compulsion; for God loves a cheerful giver" (2 Cor. 9:7).

There are many emotional hooks being used in the Christian world. Each has its own impaling urgency and stinging guilt. Starving babies, lost souls, battered women, terrorized villagers, unemployed fathers. Needs, needs—and every one vitally important.

Meanwhile, cheerful givers are on the verge of extinction. Our survival is dependent on pulling away, getting in touch with the Spirit within, and discovering the amount of joyful, volitional energy that God has prepared in us to meet a particular need. It is here, too, where we learn that even giving is a gift from God. A gift to us for a needy world. And it is always joyful.

# ON LOSING VIRTUE

It was front-page news, the biggest happening to hit town in recent memory. Rev. Jairus, the distinguished pastor of Capernaum First Church, actually had fallen on his knees in the dust before an uneducated Galilean teacher, begging. A parent, even a dignified one, will do desperate things when his child is dying. Rev. Jairus publicly humbled himself, pleading for the life of his daughter. And the Teacher agreed to heal her. This was no small event.

The crowds surged toward the Jairus home as people pushed and shoved to get a decent spot to view the spectacle. Suddenly the Teacher halted in the middle of the road. Turning around, he asked: "Who touched my clothes?" An absurd question when the masses are pressing hard upon you.

But the Teacher persisted. "Someone has touched me." It was not the ordinary jostling of crowds. It was an intentional pull on his robe, an insistent tug. He had felt this touch a thousand times before from people who wanted something from him. Someone had grabbed his garment, intruded upon him, and he felt the drain. "Virtue has gone out of me," he said.

*Master, I know the feeling. When I'm on my way to meet with an important person (like a potential donor) and a homeless person grabs my arm, insisting on talking to me right then with no concern for my time, no consideration for the harm that might be caused by my delay, it drains my energy. Care and compassion and other virtues leave me.*

*Impatience and irritation rush in. I want to respond with a quick handout or some equally demeaning put-off.*

It was a poor person, of course, who emerged trembling from the crowd. A woman with an incurable bleeding sore. A social outcast, impatient, clutching. She wanted a fix, and she got it by grabbing onto Jesus. He felt the drain. The woman was cured but Jesus lost virtue—perhaps a decline in his compassion or a twinge of impatience. Whatever, it was a clear signal to him that he must stop immediately regardless of the gravity of the situation at Jairus's home. Cure without personal care was not the Father's way. He must not go on.

*But Master, shouldn't I honor the commitments I've made to others? I need to respect their time. If I allow the urgent intrusions of poor people to control my schedule, I'll become known as irresponsible and undependable. I must maintain my priorities. Isn't that right?*

She knelt before him, healed but not heard. Then the Teacher listened. The woman's story was one of misery, alienation, and desperation. It was a story that touched the Teacher's heart. Too long a story for the anxious disciples. Horribly long for the Jairus family. But there was no rushing the woman. No expediting, no referring.

The Teacher listened attentively until the woman knew she was understood and cared for deeply. Only then he spoke. He affirmed the woman as a person of deep faith. He proclaimed that it was *her* faith—not some magical power in his robe—that healed her. His words brought wholeness to her wounded spirit, healing far deeper than a physical cure. Then the Teacher, full of virtue, continued on to the Jairus home.

But it was too late. The worst already had happened. A runner broke through the crowd bearing the tragic news. "The child just died." Rev. Jairus was stunned. The disciples were outraged. The crowd began to murmur, "If only . . . if only."

*I understand, Master, why it is important to personally care for the needy ones. But it seems unwise to lose such an important opportunity. Maybe I've helped a homeless family find food and lodging, but I've had to cancel an appointment with a busy person whose influence could do a great deal for the poor. What if I can't reschedule the appointment? What if a greater harm has been done?*

But the Teacher was calm. He wasn't affected by the outcry. Although the bleeding woman was not on his planned itinerary, he did not suppress the signals of diminishing virtue. He did not rationalize giving a quick cure just because his day was a busy one. He did things the Father's way. He knew whatever coincidences now had to be orchestrated, whatever supernatural events arranged or perceptions altered, the Father would attend to these details.

"Don't lose faith," he encouraged the grief stricken and the morally outraged. "She isn't really dead." Some jeered. The mourners wailed. They had seen the dead girl, and they knew that an opportunity was forever lost. But the few who believed that one can never lose by doing things the Father's way were invited into the child's bedroom for a behind-the-scene glimpse of an invisible reality. One of the men there learned the lesson and said it again for us in a letter: "Make every effort to add to your faith virtue" (2 Peter 1:5).

# A CHRISTMAS TRADITION

Once there was a wise and loving father who wanted to teach his children the blessings and benefits of sharing. At Christmas time, he proposed a unique plan. He would make this Christmas the best ever if the children agreed to one condition: each of them would select one of their nicest presents and give it to a poor child. The children eagerly assented.

When Christmas morning came, the children raced downstairs to see what wonderful presents awaited them. Just as their father promised, there was a marvelous array of toys beneath the Christmas tree. When the excitement died down, each child selected one of their gifts to take to a poor child. It was not an easy decision, because all the toys were new and exciting. Nonetheless, the children had given their word. And, after all, they knew there were many other toys to keep for their own.

Giving, the children found, was more fun than they expected. There was something in the smiles of the poor children, their unexpected joy, which was strangely like receiving another gift—a special kind of gift. The children agreed that this giving would make a wonderful Christmas tradition.

After several years of giving toys (which were becoming quite expensive), one of the wealthy children suggested that it might be better to stock a playhouse and invite poor children to come over and play. This way everyone could enjoy the toys and play together. The children all agreed to try it.

As the years passed, the children saw that some of the poor children coming to the playhouse did not treat the toys carefully. It was especially disturbing to see older toys (which had nostalgic value) become worn and broken. So the children decided to lock up the playhouse. It was open only when it could be carefully supervised. By now there was an enormous number of expensive toys for which they felt responsible.

Childhood slipped away and adulthood overtook the children. But Christmas remained an important time for the family. Of special significance was the tradition that their father had initiated many years before. Of course they did not actually place gifts in the playhouse anymore. But they did continue to chip in money each year to maintain and secure the playhouse, which by this time had become a valuable toy museum.

On Christmas morning, after all the gifts were opened, the grown children went out to the playhouse. They unlocked it and reminisced about their childhood. Each toy brought back memories of those special days when they used to share and play with the poor children. And they remembered how wonderful Christmas used to be.

# THE TRULY WORTHY POOR

$P$eople with a heart to serve others want to know that their gifts are invested wisely. At least I do. I don't want my alms squandered by the irresponsible and the ungrateful. And since I'm often in a position to determine who will or will not receive assistance, I've attempted to establish criteria to judge the worthiness of potential recipients.

*A truly worthy poor woman:* Is a widow more than sixty-five years old living alone in substandard housing; does not have a family or relatives to care for her. Has no savings and cannot work; has an income inadequate for basic needs. Is a woman of prayer and faith, never asks anyone for anything but only accepts with gratitude what people bring her; is not cranky.

*A truly worthy poor young man:* Is out of school, unemployed but not living off his mother. Diligently applies for jobs every day; accepts gratefully any kind of work for any kind of pay. Does not smoke, drink, or use drugs; attends church regularly. Will not manipulate for gain either for himself or his family; is dependable and morally pure. Does not act "cool" or "hip" like his peers on the street. Has pride in himself and is confident; may sleep in alleys but is always clean and shaved.

*A truly worthy poor young woman:* Lives in public housing (only temporarily). Has illegitimate children conceived prior to Christian conversion; is now celibate. Tithes her welfare check and food stamps; is a high school dropout but manages well with limited resources. Places a high value on education and nutrition for her children. Walks everywhere (grocery store, church, school, welfare office) with her children to save bus fare and keeps her sparsely furnished home spotless. Occasionally runs out of food by the end of the month, but will not beg for "handouts." Will not accept more than twenty-five dollars per month in help from friends even if her children are hungry because this violates welfare rules.

*A truly worthy poor family:* Is devout, close-knit. Has a responsible father working long hours at minimum wage wherever he can find work. Has a mother who makes the kids obey, washes clothes by hand, and will not buy any junk food. Lives in overcrowded housing; will not accept welfare or food stamps even when neither parent can find work. Always pays the bills on time; has no automobile. Has kids that do not whine or tell lies.

I want to serve truly worthy poor people. The problem is they are hard to find. Someone on our staff thought he remembered seeing one back in '76 but can't remember for sure. Someone else reminded me that maybe to be truly poor means to be prideless, impatient, manipulative, desperate, grasping at every straw, and clutching the immediate with little energy left for future plans. But truly worthy? Are any of us *truly* worthy?

# WHO SINNED HERE?

"Who sinned?" the disciples asked him. A tragedy like this doesn't just happen—it's caused. The man was born blind. It couldn't be his fault, could it? It must be something his parents did. Perhaps venereal disease. Or incest. That causes blindness sometimes. If we can get to the root cause of this, maybe we can find the key to its prevention. Or at least we can see it for what it is: God's judgment upon sin.

A homeless family. Destitute. Wandering the city streets looking for shelter, any shelter, to brace against the night chill. "Who sinned here, Lord?" Why were they evicted? Was it the father's drinking that made him lose his job? Are they just irresponsible, poor money managers? Perhaps we should check them out before we open our church to them for a place of shelter.

Hungry people starving in Ethiopia. Women with no milk left in their breasts, babies dying in their arms. Do tragedies like this just happen or are they caused? Is it drought? But why do they stream by the thousands into these desolate desert places? They flee civil war, you say. Their government sells grain to the Russsians in exchange for guns. These people starve because their sinful leaders engage in bloody political power struggles. "Is this who sinned here, Lord?"

"No," Jesus answers. "His blindness has nothing to do with his sins or his parents's sins. He is blind so that God's power may be seen at work in him."

Blindness, homelessness, hunger. Although there may be discernible causes and people to blame for the painful events of human history, these events are also opportunities for the glory of God to break through. In the midst of human misery, healing and hospitality and sharing are visible manifestations of the kingdom that has come. And the essential method of that kingdom is *personal touching*.

Is Jesus uninterested in "the bigger picture?" Surely he is concerned about mass prevention and not just individual cures. Certainly there is a need to understand cause and effect relationships, how personal and corporate sin impact people.

Yet for some reason Jesus directs our attention to a Samaritan who binds up a victim of violence rather than to a founder of a neighborhood crime watch program. He chooses to show us his kingdom by personally feeding a hungry multitude rather than examining their motives or teaching them budgeting. He heals sick men and women and children without instructing them in preventive medicine.

Why is this? Perhaps he knows the tendency of his followers to use our knowledge, our cause and effect theories, to pronounce judgment upon the suffering ones instead of healing them. He may know that we would prefer to create a program of service or champion a cause for the needy instead of risking the contagion of personal involvement. But he does not allow us to withdraw to the theoretical or theological. He forces us to feed, to clothe, to give a cup of water—to *touch* the undesirable ones. His words and his life push us to the very place that will change us and fit us for kingdom use.

It's not about root causes, he tells his followers. It's about revealing the wonder of a God who wants a personal call-me-by-name relationship with every single one of his children. Then the Master makes a little mud pack and applies it to the man's sightless eyes. And gives him unique instructions to find his way to the Pool of Siloam and wash there.

Oh, how everyone did marvel and praise God when the man came up seeing! Everyone that is, except the responsible religious people who immediately set about checking the validity of the man's condition and the biblical soundness of Jesus' method of healing.

## PART SIX

# When Old Men Dream Dreams

# I WILL POUR OUT MY SPIRIT

I maneuvered my way through the piles of junk heaped in his front yard and porch. Inside I could hear the TV playing loudly. His doorbell didn't appear to ring so I knocked loudly on the rickety aluminum screen door. Emerging through the clutter of what used to be a dining room came Mr. Boyles. He was wearing boxer shorts and a sagging athletic shirt that covered maybe half of his hairy gray chest. I introduced myself as his soon-to-be neighbor and told him that I would be building our new home (and several others) on the vacant land across the street from him. A mixture of surprise and disbelief registered on his face. He muttered a few apologetic words about his appearance, then proceeded to tell me how bad the neighborhood was. He made some passing comment about the decaying condition of his house and then, with a broad, warm smile, extended his hand to welcome me to the neighborhood.

Mr. Boyles was a widower, I later learned, and a reformed alcoholic. He had lived alone for a number of years. He could have retired from his city job years ago but needed to stay busy to stay alive. He used to be a city planner, he told me, and designed whole communities. At one time he drew up a subdivision plan for the twenty acres across the street from his house with the hope that he could develop it. That was when he was a much younger man and his life was full of possibilities. It was before he was replaced by younger professionals, before his self-confidence slipped away and before his heart bypass surgery. The decline of the neighborhood paralleled his own decline. The mounting stacks of old doors, concrete blocks, and used fixtures that filled his yard were the gravestones of abandoned dreams—sad reminders of an old man's creativity devoid of energizing hope.

Peggy and I had scarcely broken ground when Mr. Boyles came visiting. He questioned us on the arrangement of rooms, the pitch of the roof, the size of the screened-in porch and dozens of other details. "Boy, this is going to be nice," he said at least a dozen times. Over the next three months he became our resident consultant, offering free advice, talking endlessly about his city planning days and the ideas he once had for an addition to his house. "But it ain't worth nothin' now," he would say. "I ought to bulldoze it." Gradually however, we noticed Mr. Boyles said more constructive things about his house. Things like needing to get rid of some of his junk and building a retaining wall to stop an erosion problem. He even ventured a hesitant request to borrow our trailer to "do a little hauling." I noticed a load of topsoil being dumped in his front yard one morning. He spent all weekend shoveling and raking and seeding, creating lawn where once there had been weeds and debris.

By the time Peggy and I moved into our new home, several other houses were out of the ground. Teams of volunteers arrived each Saturday morning to build charming small homes for poor families. Middle-income couples eagerly watched contractors turn their blue-printed fantasies into reality. And Mr. Boyles observed with great intensity as the urban wasteland across the street became transformed into a vibrant community. A decaying city street was becoming a vigorous mixed-income neighborhood. It was a vision, materializing before our eyes. A vision authored of God, planted in our hearts, now being shared by twenty-eight families who would soon be new homeowners. It was a vision that was causing an old man to hope once again.

> In the last days, God says,
>> I will pour out my Spirit on all people.
> Your sons and daughters will prophesy,
>> your young men will see visions,
>>> and your old men will dream dreams.
>>>> (*Acts 2:17–19*)

In the heart of the city, the Creator Spirit moves, and I watch in amazement. Young (and not so young) professional couples are choosing to leave comfort and status and, like prophetic beacons, plant their lives among the poor. Visionaries who catch glimpses of an invisible kingdom paint their word pictures for those who have eyes to see. The diverse members of God's family, richly equipped with every talent needed to create new life in the city, authenticate with their lives the reality of that kingdom. And old men—apathetic, dying old men—begin to dream dreams.

Last Saturday afternoon Mr. Boyles flagged me down as I rode by on the tractor. He wanted a bump in his driveway graded so a truck could deliver his new workshop to the back yard of his attractive little home.

# A DREAM DEFERRED

I scarcely remember the phone call. A man with a New York City accent said something about working a deal. He wanted me to send folks to his store who needed food. He struck me as another fast talking entrepreneur hoping to make a buck off the needs of poor people, and I expressed no interest in making a "deal." I promptly dismissed the conversation from my mind.

Later, when I was looking for a suitable location for a non-profit food store, I walked into a small corner grocery store in one of the poorer sections of the community. The building was drab, and plaster was falling from the walls and ceiling. The stock consisted of Cokes, candy, cigarettes, Twinkies, and a sparse supply of white bread and milk. Less than one-quarter of the small building was in use. The rest was stacked with broken coolers and rusting metal shelves.

Behind the counter was a stumpy little man with a round face and a balding gray head. He wore a T-shirt, and carried a .38 caliber pistol strapped high on his rotund waist. Behind him, leaning against the counter in plain view, was a shotgun. He fit the stereotype of a hard-nosed shopkeeper who knew how to do business in the ghetto.

The man greeted me abruptly. There was something vaguely familiar about his voice. I introduced myself and told him that we wanted to provide nutritious, affordable food for the poor in our community. Our plan was to get favorable buying status with major grocery stores and to convince churches to share their food pantry supplies. For distribution, we needed a location in the heart of the poorest part of the neighborhood.

The man listened to my proposal intently and expressed neither surprise nor resentment when I mentioned our interest in purchasing his store building. Then he began to ask questions. They were probing questions intended to get at underlying motives. When at last he seemed satisfied that my desire was for service rather than opportunism, he began to speak from his heart.

He reminded me of his phone call to me four years before. He pulled out old correspondence which he had written in vain to various religious, business, and political leaders. Over and over again he had asked for help in finding a means to bring healthy, fair-priced food into the community.

"This has been my dream for fifteen years," he said, his eyes moist and intense. "I have never found the way to do it."

Yes, he would like to sell his store to us. He could retire with the joy of knowing that his dream was being fulfilled. Well concealed behind the menacing, abrasive exterior of this shopkeeper was a compassionate heart yearning for righteousness. He told me the story, from his own Jewish tradition, of Moses— how he was permitted to look over into Canaan but was prevented from entering with the people. Likening himself to Moses, he added, "God is allowing me to see my dream come true. Maybe he will let me walk a ways into the promised land with you."

# WELFARE REDEFINED

**wel·fare** | ′wel-,fa(ə)re | *n* 1: the state of doing well esp. in respect to good fortune, happiness, well-being, or prosperity

Welfare. Such a positive word as Webster defines it. But its meaning has changed in recent years. It has become despised. It evokes feelings of anger and resentment. It is the generic term for a system that destroys people.

Take people who are able and strong. Place them in the wealthiest land on earth. Surround them with unparalleled opportunity. Then pay them not to work, not to strive, not to achieve. Pay them to accept nonproductivity as a way of life. Agree to subsidize their families with food, shelter, health care, and money if the fathers will leave.

Do this for two or three generations and see what you produce. You will have a people who are unmotivated and dependent, whose hopes and dreams rise no higher than their subsidies—a people who have lost the work ethic, who have learned that others will take responsibility for them and who therefore assert little discipline or control over their own lives. You will have emasculated their men, making them expendable and unnecessary to their families' existence. You will have created a generation of prideless, fatherless youth who believe that receiving and taking is better than working and investing. And when you have seen the hope disappear from the eyes of the young, you can be sure you have developed an effective formula for the destruction of a people. We call it welfare.

It is time to redefine this word. It is time to create a system that will produce "a state of faring well" for the people who have not fared so well in our land. It is time to institute a system that affirms that every person has something worthwhile to contribute, that the "more blessed" position of giving is to be shared by all those created in God's image.

Take an inner-city neighborhood largely populated by poor, dependent people. Salt it with hopeful, energetic, visionary Christians who share their lives and dreams with others. Secure the cooperation of churches in the community to combine food cupboards, clothes closets, and hearts in a unified commitment to responsible caring. Establish an agreement of exchange: a bag of groceries for a cleaned up lot; a shirt for a mopped hall; a dress for two hours in the nursery. Let the "haves" work in partnership with the "have-nots," each bringing something of value to contribute. Develop a system of reciprocity that gives poor people the dignity of earning and produces in the giver a sense of indebtedness and gratitude.

Let the system be small and manageable so that accountability and integrity can be maintained. Let it be a personal system in which rich and poor touch each other's lives, where their values collide so that both are changed. And when you see pride return to the eyes of the young, and when the affluent offer with appreciation fair compensation for a job well done, you will know that you have created a model of community that is worthy to be called *welfare*.

# KINGDOM EFFICIENCY

**ef·fi·cien·cy** i-'fish-ən-sē | *n* 1 : the capacity to produce desired results with a minimum expenditure of energy, time, money, or materials.

There is something inside me that makes me smile when I see a well-run operation: phones answered professionally, details observed, appointments kept promptly, systems flowing with logical consistency. The competent execution of a well-designed plan is a thing of beauty for me. My love of efficiency is woven inextricably into the fabric of my personality.

Recently the staff of Family Consultation Service discussed relocating our offices. Our two rooms in a small urban church are seriously overcrowded. A constant stream of kids, church folks, and people from the community make it increasingly difficult to perform necessary administrative tasks. Some days seem like one continuous interruption. "It's impossible to get any work done at the office," I say to Peggy in frustration. It violates my sense of responsibility to see my desk piled high with unanswered correspondence, unopened mail, and the notes from unreturned phone calls.

My efficiency-loving mind tells me the solution is in the system. I envision a building away from church traffic. It has ample office space, phones, and meeting rooms. We are centralized under one roof instead of operating out of homes and cars and brief cases. We better coordinate our communication and cut down on impromptu drop-ins. And I get some work done.

Work? What is my work? Is organizational efficiency really the bottom line? Should a clean desk and a balanced financial report by the *fifth of the month* be my priority? Is my job well done when my schedule book clicks with precision and the minutia of details are carefully covered? This would satisfy my need for order and control, but what about the kingdom of God?

The fundamental building blocks of the kingdom are relationships. Not programs, systems, or productivity. But inconvenient, time-consuming, intrusive relationships. The kingdom is built on personal involvements that disrupt schedules and drain energy. When I enter into redemptive relationships with others, I lose much of my "capacity to produce desired results with a minimum expenditure of energy, time, money, or materials." In short, relationships sabotage my efficiency. A part of me dies. Is this perhaps what our Lord meant when he said we must lay down our lives for each other?

If efficiency is a value in God's kingdom, surely it has a different definition. The one who orchestrates history doesn't seem to be in a hurry. God doesn't seem to need closure at the end of each day. Perhaps if one has an eternity in which to accomplish one's work, it's not so important to handle every urgent detail that arises. Kingdom efficiency must have an eternal perspective.

How then can we earthbound ones evaluate our own level of kingdom efficiency? Obedience is the only trustworthy measure I have found. I know I am called to love people and, in a special sense, poor people. Since it is impossible to schedule their calamities, I must remain open to their interruptions. The seductive appeal of order would draw me away from my call. God's peace must be learned in the midst of disturbance. Disruptions are his reminders that people are more important than programs and that the ordering of my life is his business. Perhaps in the disarray of human relationships he will reveal the true meaning of efficiency.

# LOSING WITH GOD

It was a wonderfully adventurous opportunity. Business people, consultants, and other bright Christians all concurred. A pallet manufacturing operation in the heart of the city would create labor intensive jobs and develop the work habits of our young men. Few skills were required. An empty warehouse was available. There was a ready market for wooden shipping pallets.

It was agreed then. The time, dollars, and human resources were committed. Leases were signed and equipment moved into place. An eight-man crew was hired from the neighborhood. Two good managers and an experienced consultant jumped into action. Truck loads of lumber arrived, and the sounds of saws and staple guns filled the urban air. It was right. We knew it. We could feel it in our spirits.

We cheered when the first pallet rolled off the line. Soon our large flatbed truck was stacked high and pulling out of the yard—our first shipment to our first major customer.

We discovered that sawing up tons of hard wood produced considerable sawdust. No problem. A vacuum system would save many hours of shoveling and carrying. We invested in a large commercial blower to suck the sawdust from the saws and blow it into an outside dumpster. It would pay for itself in no time.

As soon as we switched the blower on we discovered a major flaw. It blew dust everywhere—like blowing on a saucer of flour. A huge mushroom cloud of foul-smelling, sour oak dust rose from our little plant and drifted over the community. We raced for the breaker to quickly and permanently shut the blower down.

The blower was just the beginning. Soon nails were tearing teeth out of one-hundred-dollar saw blades. Employees stapled themselves to pallets. Fingers were cut and crushed by high-speed machines. There was no time to slow down. Four hundred and fifty pallets *must* roll out each day to keep up with the orders.

Fighting and absenteeism became acute. But there was no time for counseling. Turnover approached 100 percent in the first eight weeks. Consultants recommended changes. A compressor went out and production came to a halt. Eight men stood idle as two managers raced to find a replacement.

A mountain of scrap wood climbed heavenward. Trash trucks increased their sawdust runs. New consultants. More changes. Someone drove the forklift through the side of the warehouse, collapsing the metal overhead door. Managers lost weight, and showed signs of serious fatigue. An employee slumped to the ground, unconscious, was resuscitated, and rushed to the hospital. Production had to go on. In our best days we lost five cents on every pallet we produced. We concluded it was impossible to make up our losses in volume. To survive, we needed sophisticated machinery that would eliminate most of our workers.

There comes a time when cutting one's losses and getting out is the better part of wisdom. Time has now sufficiently distanced me from the guilt and embarrassment of this fiasco to permit a bit of calm reflection. What went wrong? Why did we so miserably fail when our motives, our mission, our plans were all of high quality? Did we not listen carefully enough to God's Spirit?

Behind my questioning is the subtle heresy that God will prosper any endeavor that is done according to his will. The corollary is that whatever fails was done somehow contrary to his intentions. The error is in the assumption that perfect communion with God assures flawless performance of his will. But neither perfect communion nor flawless performance is possible for human beings.

Success, I've learned, has little to do with the performance of God's will. Sometimes we fail because of our own stupidity or shortsightedness, and we must learn lessons from our mistakes. Sometimes we fail because of someone else's failure, or because there was too much rain or too little rain. In these cases, there are no corrective lessons to be learned.

Success is not an automatic consequence of obedience. "A righteous man falls seven times and rises again" (Prov. 24:16). Saint and sinner alike must take their lumps and go on to the next risk. But for the believer there is one guarantee. We have a dependable God who made a trustworthy commitment that no matter what happens—success or failure—he will use it for our ultimate good.

## PART SEVEN

# Kingdom Playgrounds

# "WHY DO YOU WANT TO RUIN
OUR COMMUNITY?"

I was surrounded. I stood in the middle of a glass-strewn basketball court at the ruins of an inner-city school. A growing circle of unsmiling faces stared at me. Feet shifted in uneasy silence. I wished I had a friend to back me up; it was only a matter of time until a confrontation erupted.

But these were not street punks out to spill blood. The weapons they carried were not guns or knives. These people were young urban professionals. They had secured their personal pieces of urban real estate, and they were not about to yield an inch of their turf without a fight.

The conflict had begun a few months earlier when we were considering using the vacant school as a shelter for the homeless. The same week the school board was to give its decision, the school mysteriously caught fire and burned to the ground. The school board, wanting to put the empty land to some redemptive use, offered it to Family Consultation Service (FCS) as a location on which to build low-income housing.

Several young urban professionals who were renovating homes in the neighborhood challenged the school board's plan. They organized a political assault to pressure the board to rescind its contract with FCS. A sealed-bid auction was arranged to settle the matter, with the land going to the highest bidder. As it turned out, there were only two interested parties: the young urban professionals and FCS. When the envelopes were opened and the bids read, FCS's offer was high by *one dollar!*

Even then the conflict wasn't over. The losing bidders accused the school board of collusion and threatened legal action. Smear and fear tactics were used to intimidate us. The outcry was heard throughout the community and even reached city hall. Nonetheless, the ownership of the property was transferred to FCS.

Now on the basketball court, for the first time I saw our opponents, eye-to-eye, neighbor-to-neighbor. The crowd had grown to twenty-five or more. As we stared at each other, I wondered if there was somewhere in their angry midst a compassionate person.

"Why do you want to ruin our community?" The silence was finally broken, and a reservoir of stored-up emotions poured out. There was fear, anger, resentment, and more fear. These people were homeowners, risk-taking pioneers who had staked out their claim on the urban frontier and now saw their investment threatened.

They were not mean people. They were hard-working, self-respecting, even church-going folk. They had nothing against the poor; they emphasized this again and again. It was only that smaller homes and low-income neighbors would slow the rise in property values. The (necessary) displacement of the poor from the community was an economic issue, not a moral one. No one wanted to be unkind, they assured me. They just wanted to build a stable, good community.

The confrontation represented a classic conflict, one common to all humankind. The battle of spirit versus mammon was being dramatized on an urban stage. People of good will were being torn in their hearts between protecting their investments and caring for their neighbors in need. It was a volatile, emotion-laden matter that forced them to decide where to place their treasures, and thus their hearts.

It is far easier to make these decisions in corporate board rooms, where one is removed from the immediacy of human survival. Financial decisions can be cleanly negotiated without the messy entanglement of social dilemmas. But on the broken concrete basketball court at this inner-city school, ordinary kindhearted people stared at a painful choice. Either they would open their hearts and their community to the less fortunate and risk lower property values, or they would choose profit as their preferred value and fight to protect their treasure.

I knew that their choices really were not being made on the basketball court. They were being formed by a thousand value-laden messages from our culture that bombard them daily. And formed too, of course, by the quiet constant voice of the Spirit.

Last Saturday we celebrated the completion of the first small house built by people of faith on the school's land. Someone has threatened to torch the house. Two of our most outspoken opponents have put their homes on the market. Across the street a middle-aged couple has decided that loving one's neighbor is a higher value than real estate profit, and they have begun to build a new home.

# DID I REALLY SAY THAT?

He was a pushy little man, a man who learned early that to get ahead you have to look out for yourself. Rather than fight the jostling crowds that pressed for a glimpse of the Teacher, Zack figured out his own strategy. No one else had seen the low hanging limb of a large sycamore that stretched directly above the Teacher's route. The view was excellent. Zack smiled. His own private box seat above the crowds. Perfect.

What followed was beyond his most self-centered fantasies. Public recognition by the famous Teacher. An invitation to personally host the Master in the privacy of his own home. Incredible—and life-changing. By the time the day ended, this rich, devious little man had repented of his fraudulent business dealings, committed himself to a four-to-one restitution plan, and pledged one-half of his wealth to the poor. No one who knew Zack would deny that he was truly converted.

It wasn't until Jesus left and the ecstasy of this memorable day subsided that Zack began to understand the implications of his commitment. Four-to-one on every dishonest deal. That was a lot of money. There were a few big rip-offs looming large on Zack's conscience. These he must repay fourfold without delay. But what about all those shady transactions based on misinformation and half-truth? What about the unethical, if not illegal, schemes pulled on the unsuspecting?

Four-to-one on all of them would virtually wipe him out. Plus half of his wealth to the poor? What a joke! He wouldn't have any disposable wealth left to divide. He'd have to sell his summer home in the mountains and most of his investment property in the city. The show camels and his prize breeding rams would have to go too. Zack couldn't remember if he'd said 50 percent of his net worth before or after restitution. For the first time the issue of tithing on net versus gross income arose in Zack's mind. For the first time he began to question the practicality of his commitment to Christ.

Peggy and I recently sold our home in Grant Park to build a more modest home in adjacent Ormewood Park. Our purpose was to begin ministry among the poor of this community. We made a commitment to adjust our lifestyle downward so we could better blend into our inner-city neighborhood and free up more of our resources for kingdom work.

As soon as we started sketching floor plans, however, a conflict of values arose. Room sizes, lighting fixtures, floor coverings, cabinetry—each decision required a value judgment. Peggy and I have a well-developed appreciation for the finer things in life. We admire rich wood finishes and fine craftsmanship. We are also called to invest ourselves among people in need. You can see the conflict. We could do without a garage but a charming work shed would be nice. The 50' times 150' lot is OK, but attractive landscaping is important. Just one—or maybe two—really nice light fixtures. And good durable vinyl that will require minimal care.

In this way we rationalized our way through solid wood doors, better faucets, the second bath and central air—the pull of privilege winning consistently over the call to conserve. With each choice came the struggle to pry our fingers from our tightly held possessions. It became frightfully clear just how much we are attached to our comfort and convenience. To move down once you have grown accustomed to "the good life," we discovered, is unbelievably difficult.

How did you do it, Zack? How did your commitment hold up? Did you end up deferring your giving? Did you retain control of your wealth through "dedicated" funds? Did you spiritualize away your commitment into "willingness of heart" rather than actual disbursement of cash?

Tell us you made it, Zack. Be our example of a rich man who broke free from the grasp of greed. Tell us you won the struggle with mammon and abandoned yourself to the Christ who touched you. Tell us, Zack, that we can be liberated from the power of privilege.

# KINGDOM PLAYGROUNDS

There they sit, row after row of remarkably gifted grown-ups. Dressed in proper Sunday attire, they are waiting. Waiting for the minister to step to the microphone with words to ignite them. Hoping that this Sunday he will challenge them to more than a capital funds campaign for the new family life center. They wait, these talented ones, for words to stir them, to drive them from their comfort to challenges worthy of their best. Perhaps today they will hear the call to tasks of greater significance than their own personal success or the growth of their church.

An architect, a CPA, a surgeon, and seven other professionals file down the center aisle. They bow for prayer, then dutifully fan out with offering plates to collect a cut of the profits from the marketplace. With the exception of a CEO from an international trade organization who reads the morning scripture, ushering is the most noticeable role that lay leaders fill.

Less visible are the real estate developers, insurance brokers, and educators who serve on church committees. But there they sit, a people with the nature and the gifts of the Divine, fully equipped with every skill and ability necessary to tackle the complex problems of the world. Although domesticated by their culture, they long for the courage to throw off the obligations of consumerism and spend themselves for the God who has called them.

Outside the stained glass windows, beyond the parking lot, toward the skyline where most of the gifted ones make their living, there is a place that churns with the challenges of eternity. It is the burgeoning center into which the peoples and perplexities of our shrinking globe pour. A place filled with adventure and intrigue, it calls out for the full investment of every gift entrusted to God's chosen ones. It is the city.

Amidst the chaos of its crowds and the ominous power of its structures, there exists small, nearly invisible pockets of vigorous, healthy growth. In old storefronts and empty warehouses of decaying communities, gifted ones are finding each other. Called from different places by the same voice, they are joining hands and hearts to take on the overwhelming problems of the city. In the process they are creating kingdom playgrounds.

Strange things happen in kingdom playgrounds. Adults become children and learn to play again. They bring their best tools and talents (the toys of the kingdom) and dream together. They invent ingenious methods to feed and clothe the poor, methods that enhance rather than destroy. They create new economies in destitute neighborhoods, and build homes and businesses and hope where despair has reigned.

In these kingdom playgrounds, impossibilities become probabilities and visions become reality. Here children discover the secrets of how kingdom magic really works.

In kingdom playgrounds God's children play with great intensity. At times they may grow weary, but they are never bored. They learn that their gifts, which they once thought were useful only for making money in the marketplace, are actually the exact abilities needed to work in God's kingdom. In these unlikely places, God's children discover that the serious work of eternity is simply the joyful employment of the talents they desire most to express.

The gifted ones are standing up now. Doctrine has been masterfully restated, the large Bible on the pulpit has been closed, a proper benediction pronounced. The one-hundred-member choir sings an impeccably harmonious AMEN and all the responsible, gifted adults file out. They return once again to their adult obligations, not knowing that they were never created to be adults anyway: "Truly I say to you, unless you turn and become like children, you will never enter the Kingdom of Heaven" (Matt. 18:3).

# IT BELONGS TO GOD

**corban** ′kȯ(ə)r-,ban *n*: an ancient Hebrew practice of dedicating property to God, thus removing it from secular disposition, while still retaining ownership. Literally: it belongs to God.

It was an ingenious invention, really. Corban was something like a tax incentive plan conceived by the religious leadership. A donor could make a contract with the church to dedicate certain of his holdings to the Lord but still use them for collateral in business dealings. Like most religious schemes, corban fell into abuse and soon took precedence over other more fundamental commands of God. It was on this point that Jesus offered some unwelcome words to the church leadership.

"You have a clever way of rejecting God's law in order to uphold you own teaching," the Master said. "You teach that if a person has something he could use to help his father and mother but says 'This is corban' (which means, it belongs to God), he is excused from helping his father and mother. In this way the teaching you pass on to others cancels out the word of God" (Mark 7:9–13).

In other words, to commit wealth in any form to God and then refuse to allow its use for those things God commands is sin. Shrewd sin. But sin nonetheless.

The practice of corban has surfaced in various forms throughout church history. It is a symptom of the struggle of redeemed yet fallen humanity, caught between two worlds. Corban indicates the extent to which religious people have taken control over the kingdom they call God's.

The church of which we all are a part has not escaped this tension. We too are pulled between the instinct for self-preservation and the yearning to spend our security on the intangibles of kingdom reality. And being wealthy beyond historic comparison, the church is not immune from the influences of contemporary wisdom. We have learned to invest God's resources in inflation-proof real estate and to protect his options with legal documents. It is hard to imagine how much of the assets of the kingdom are reserved in the endowments, dedicated funds, and certificates of deposit of the Western church. The Hebrews called it corban. We call it good stewardship.

We endow ministries that serve our needs, taking care to spend only the interest earnings while making the principle available to GM and Xerox for their operating capital. Meanwhile the poor in nearby inner-city churches are scattered for lack of shepherding, because their pastors must work two jobs to survive. This is corban.

We build magnificent holy places for our weekly worship. But when these houses that we call God's are for our exclusive feeding while those without daily bread remain outside, this is corban. When those who have no place to lay their head are excluded from what we call God's sanctuary, it is corban. It is corban when we dam up the flow of our Lord's resources in restricted reservoirs against his kingdom's future needs, when these resources are required to provide employment and shelter for the very ones he affectionately calls "the least of these."

The Church is the only institution which, without irresponsibility, can expend all its resources on great and lavish outbursts of compassion. It is ordained to give itself away, yet without loss. The Church, above all earthly symbols, bears the responsibility for declaring in the outpouring of resources, the utter dependability of God. To preserve its life is to lose it.

But Master, we have no money left to feed the hungry or clothe the naked or shelter the homeless. Our benevolence fund is completely used up. The restricted funds? Well, we want to be responsible stewards. Of course, all of it is really yours. It *is* corban.

## PART EIGHT

# When Losing Is Winning

# THE DEATH OF MRS. BAILEY

The death of Mrs. Bailey brought a mixture of sadness and relief to our family. Sadness because we lost a close friend; relief because she was a demanding responsibility. Mrs. Bailey was an elderly woman confined to a wheelchair, unable to clip her own toenails or wash her own hair. For five years Peggy had shopped for Mrs. Bailey's groceries and taken her to the bank and the doctor. Mrs. Bailey spent her holidays and other special days in our home. And in the end our sadness at her death was as much for the tragedy of her life as it was for the loss of a close friend.

To the end, Mrs. Bailey would not move from her home. Although the neighborhood became dangerous and she was chronically afraid, her fear of leaving was greater than her fear of remaining. Her only place of security was behind the dead bolts and drawn blinds of the house that held a lifetime of memories.

Day after day Mrs. Bailey sat in her wheelchair, lights dimmed, tending to her private affairs. Her affairs? Stacking old bills and years of cancelled checks on a dining room table no longer used for eating. Folding and neatly storing paper bags, torn pieces of old sheets, rubber bands, stockings and undergarments that were long since retired from active duty. Mrs. Bailey threw away nothing, absolutely nothing, except refuse itself. Hoarding had become her way of life. Dust and decay were her unwanted but constant companions.

It had not always been this way. Once her house was full of life. The wind blew through curtains at open windows. There was laughter and giving. A family invested itself, lavishing love on a child, toiling happily for the joys of the moment and the dreams of the future.

Then Mr. Bailey died. Mrs. Bailey and her son clung to each other for comfort. Gradually her selfless love became controlling, suffocating. A life-giving relationship became deadly. There was hard work. Bad financial times. More clutching. The son married and moved away—another loss. Neighbors moved too. She was now alone. Sturdier locks were installed on the doors; the blinds were lowered. She became fiercely independent. She conserved money, electricity, papers, cardboard boxes.

More years slipped away. Mrs. Bailey saved more and more of what she had less and less need for. Her health began to fail. She obtained a wheelchair to conserve physical energy and prevent falls. She ceased to spend. Her growing savings accounts and insurance policies were no longer a comfort, and she begrudged every expense of living. Food became as distasteful to her as the thought of paying for it. She even conserved her love, meting out only what she was sure would be returned.

Mrs. Bailey hoarded every possession but life itself, and now that was gone. But her death actually occurred years before her heart stopped beating. Her death was signaled when she first began to clutch at life. "If you would save your life, you will lose it; But if you lose your life for my sake, you will find it" (Matt 16:25).

The church is engaged in a similar struggle. We are in a death drift that moves us from serving to preserving. We feel it carrying us along. Our spontaneous fellowship soon becomes a program. Bearing one another's burdens becomes a budget line item. Self-sacrificing friends become paid professionals with titles (counselor, minister, director) and salary packages, longevity guarantees, and retirement benefits. Our meeting places turn into "holy places" with stained glass, polished oak, and locks. Taking "no thought for tomorrow" becomes sentimental rhetoric as we build bigger barns and amass insurance and endowments and reserve funds against the unpredictable events of our future.

But the church has no future. We have only the present. In this present moment we must spend, lavish, and give away our tomorrows for the sake of his kingdom today. In short, we must die. Today. That is the only way to save our lives. The church is called to live at Golgotha. If perchance tomorrow morning we discover that our depleted spirits have a new supply of energy, that the emptied offering plate is full once again, and from sacrificial dreams whole new dimensions of life have burst forth, then we will begin to understand something of what the resurrection is about. On the other side of death, each death, stands our risen Lord. And he beckons us.

# THAT THEY MAY BE ONE

He only had begun to teach them about the ways of the kingdom when time ran out. How could this be their last get-together when so much was yet to be learned? In the brief moments remaining, the Teacher carefully instructed them once more on how to conduct themselves as kingdom people.

This time he called it a New Commandment. (In reality, it was an old commandment to which he was about to give new meaning.) He once again told these diverse, unlikely followers that they must love each other. He was very insistent on this point, even demanding that they love "as much as I love you" (John 15:12).

When the meeting was over, the Teacher closed in prayer. "Father, make them one. Make them so much a part of each other that when one hurts, they all feel the pain. Make them inseparable, as loyal to each other as you and I are loyal to one another. May their commitment to each other be so deep and visible that there is no doubt their love is not of an earthly kind. Make them the very reflection of the kind of unity and glory we have together in heaven. Then the world will know for sure that I was sent from you. Amen" (John 17:11b–21).

Then he was gone. Taken from them in a whirlwind of events: an arrest, the cross, the resurrection, the ascension. But what he left behind was so strange and wonderful it was beyond human imagination. In the trust of a couple of commercial fishermen, an IRS agent, a political activist, a former prostitute, a doctor, a businesswoman and an assortment of mostly low-income, uneducated folk he left the keys that would open the entire world to his kingdom. He entrusted to them his New Commandment and a new power, the Holy Spirit, that would enable them to obey it. He would use them and their simple obedience as a means to reveal himself to the world. It would not be their wise words but their unusual commitment to each other that convinced the world of his deity.

The Teacher has been gone for quite some time now. In his absence some confusion has arisen. Certain of his followers have taken the position that the Great Commission is more important than the New Commandment. They have developed remarkable strategies to evangelize entire cities and nations. They have devised ways to broadcast his words from powerful satellites in the heavens. They have learned to grow successful churches by grouping together all the people who are alike. In fact, because they have become wealthy and powerful, they can do almost anything they desire to promote the kingdom.

The problem is that the active love demanded by the Teacher cannot be adequately communicated through television studios. Deep commitment to one another is not observed in proliferating the printed word. And homogeneous churches do not reflect a unity that differs from other groupings common to this world. In skipping over the tough demands of the Teacher, we have forfeited the very power which he said would prove his deity to the world.

Admittedly, it is easier to mouth loving words into a microphone than to confront someone who has offended you. It is more stimulating to do creative program planning than to wrestle through one's own self-centeredness and prejudice. Worship and fellowship in the comfort of the familiar is so much more pleasant than the hard work of laying down one's own liturgical or theological preferences for the sake of a brother or sister. And the homogeneous approach to kingdom building is marketable. It is selling well.

I suspect, however, that when all is said and done the convincing, life-changing power of the kingdom will be experienced right where the Teacher said it would be—where the lives of his diverse followers are laid down for each other. Perhaps the world will catch glimpses of his reality when:

his efficient ones are inconvenienced by the slow;
the bright ones lavish their valuable time and talents on the ignorant;
those who have much sacrifice for those who do not have enough;
those who normally separate from each other on the basis of IQ, skin tone, age, or earnings place their lives together intentionally, inseparably, for the sake of their Teacher.

# FROM WHENCE COME WARS
# AND FIGHTINGS AMONG YOU?

A young Christian, nineteen years old, watches anxiously as world tensions mount. Iran, Afghanistan, Central America: they trouble him. A presidential order requiring all draft-age males to register with the Selective Service sends him to the scriptures to study its view on war. He sincerely desires to live out the values of the kingdom, and through prayer, study, and counsel from other believers, he arrives at a decision: in obedience to the word of God, he will not register. In civil disobedience, he takes his stand for the cause of righteousness.

Another draft-age youth, also a Christian, watches the same events. He too is troubled by the suffering in the world. He is convinced that war, all war, is wrong. Yet when the order to register comes, he is caught in a tension between what seems to be two evils. He remembers the biblical injunction to obey the authorities, and he too spends hours in prayer and searching the scriptures. He seeks the counsel of older, wiser people of faith. His final decision: in obedience to the word of God he will register.

The same struggle of conscience takes place over many other serious issues. Why do Christians not agree on such important matters? Is it because some are more spiritually mature than others? Are some more hermeneutically astute and able to gain more accurate insight into the word of God? Surely

God doesn't contradict himself. What shall we do when well-meaning Christians come up with different answers from the ones God has clearly revealed to us as his truth?

Perhaps we should try to educate these ignorant ones. If they refuse to accept the truth, we can cut them off from our fellowship. Didn't Christ say, "I came not to bring peace but a sword?" (Matt. 10:34). Surely peace at any price is not the answer.

But one of the things that troubles me as I take up causes for the kingdom is this: our Lord has told us the essential I.D. for all "card-carrying" Christians is "By this shall all men know that you are my disciples, if you have love for one another" (John 13:35). There is nothing distinguishing about holding certain political positions, engaging in debates, staging protests. Whether we pledge allegiance to the moral majority or the radical minority, whether we vote Republican or Democrat (or Independent, Libertarian, or Socialist), there is no visible statement to the world about our commitment to the lordship of Christ. We may join pro- or anti-nuke, life, draft, ERA, Contra, or defense bandwagons and do so for all the right reasons, but this will not cause us to shine like lights in darkness. Such affiliations may express our convictions, but they do not set us apart as "Christ-ones."

There is only one activity so unique to this world that Christ distinguished it as the proof of his diety and of our authenticity as his followers. It is more disarming than SALT talks. It is more reconciling than Camp David peace accords, more convincing than arguments for and against abortion or gay rights, or the authority of scripture. It illuminates the minds of men and women more than Christian television or political debates, and it is not an option for a Christian. It is a command. It is love. Love of a special sort.

Unfortunately, we seldom see this love. We talk about it, but quickly abandon it in the pursuit of "rightness." Perhaps building cases for issues is much more exciting than loving each other; issues allow us to win, or at least compete. Love, on the other hand, lays down its ego, its case, its defenses for the sake of another—and that isn't fun.

And yet our Lord saw love as so vital that he spent his last night emphasizing and reemphasizing it to his disciples. He assured them (and us) that he would reveal himself to them, give his Holy Spirit to teach them, grant all that they ask, give them peace and joy, and call them his friends if they would but obey him by living out his love (John 13–15). Would it be easy? Is laying down your life easy? Yet, said Christ, this is how love is measured.

But what about the issues? Shouldn't we take stands on important issues like human rights, war, and even life itself? Of course. We must. This isn't to say that all Christians will take the same stand. As long as we are fallen and our perceptions are colored by our experience, as long as we have blind spots and different personalities (aggressive and passive, patient and impulsive, philosophical and practical, creative and rigid), we will continue coming up with different answers. We will disagree over disarmament and genetic planning, over movie-going and laetrile.

Yet somehow in the tension between the poles, God continues to work. Love leads us to an *appreciative* understanding of the unique contribution each member makes to the body of Christ, and thus the tension is creative. But without the willingness to lay aside, at least for a time, our own position in order to affirm a dissenting brother or sister, the tension will undoubtedly be destructive. I suspect that Christ is working overtime these days healing the ears (and egos) of those we have slashed in his defense. Perhaps it is time we put away our swords and began displaying the mark of "Christ-ones:" Love.

# DOWNWARD MOBILITY

A passion for excellence. Diligence. Drive. Efficiency. The competitive edge. These are the values of achievers, the essence of upward mobility and the stuff of which success is made.

Enter Jesus, the Christ. Mighty God. The Everlasting Father. Emptied. Weak. Dependent. Here to show us the way to greatness, heavenly greatness, by becoming least. King turned servant. Downwardly mobile. What sort of ethic is this?

There are those who will find it exceedingly difficult to understand, the Teacher said. Like the wealthy, successful, educated ones. But there will be a few renegades and other out-of-step people who will be given eyes to perceive the kingdom. They will listen to the homeless leader who owned one change of clothes, didn't budget to pay his taxes, and was an affront to self-respecting, responsible believers.

"Take no thought for tomorrow . . . don't worry about what you will eat or wear . . . don't lay up treasures here . . . give your coat . . . share your bread . . . lend without expecting a return." Wonderful rhetoric but highly impractical. Suicidal if taken literally—and so the reasonable folks did not take it that way.

Indeed, his teachings are suicidal for the successful. The downward mobility of the kingdom strikes at the very heart of our earthly strivings. It feels like death to let go of our diligent preparations for the next step up and the investments that insure our tomorrows. Who in their right mind would gamble away a reasonably predictable and secure future on a high-risk, intangible faith venture like the kingdom of God? A balanced portfolio makes more sense. A good mix of earthly investments with enough heavenly stock to carry us if the bottom falls out of the economy. The best of both worlds, we might say.

Jesus the Christ. Mighty God. Destitute. He says we can't have it both ways, that our security is either in God or mammon. He tells us that the servant is not greater than his master, that greatness—his and ours—is found only in servanthood, in choosing the lesser positions while yielding the better places to others. It is only in laying down our privilege, our control, our comfort for the sake of others, he says, that we can know life as he created it to be.

Heavenly hosts burst forth in hallelujahs (not tears) at the sight of their naked, helpless Creator in the straw. Heaven's best lavished on the least of earth. Glory to God, they exclaimed. The first fruits of a new world order have come, and he has revealed the values of his kingdom: vulnerability, obedience with abandon, lavish giving, faith that defies reason, volitional downward mobility.

Foolishness. God has chosen the weak to lead the strong and the foolish to confound the wise. His end? That all may know his utter dependability to care for those who will risk trusting him.

## PART NINE

# Snowflakes and Sunsets

# UP AND OUT

A young man from the inner city secures an excellent job with an expanding industrial firm. His persistence in gaining an education has paid off. Family and friends from his old neighborhood share his excitement. At first. But now he is gone. And the poverty in the city intensifies.

Boy meets girl at a little inner-city church. They fall in love. The part-time minister performs their wedding. It's a simple ceremony, but to the poor congregation it is a special occasion. The couple's combined income enables them to purchase a small home in the suburbs. Now they are gone. And the despair in the city intensifies.

A bright young woman studies the language and values of the marketplace and then ventures from the projects to market her abilities. She gets a job with a large communications corporation and soon reaps the economic benefits of the free enterprise system. Now she must live the part: her clothes, car, and apartment must reflect and reinforce her success. And she is gone too. Another bright hope for the city disappears and the darkness intensifies.

Why do they all leave? Why do they pull away from family and friends who have been their community?

For good reasons. One young person cannot earn enough to pull an extended family out of poverty. Success depends on saying no to family needs—and the estrangement begins. A young couple wanting the best for their children understandably withdraws to the safety and quality education of the suburbs. And an aspiring young woman is not likely to find in the "projects" a responsible, educated husband to share her dreams.

It all makes good sense. Who can fault this kind of courage and desire? But what about the city? The stranglehold of poverty tightens with each hope that leaves. Is there no deliverance for those who are left behind?

# TOLERABLE TARES

We were ready for a vacation. Twelve straight months of city living made the cabin toward which we headed more appealing than ever to our family. For the last few miles, Jeff and Jonathan hung over the front seat, eagerly chattering about "hitting the water." We made a right turn off the main road, then a left into the cottage drive. There, around the last bend, appeared the lake, placid and clear. The car barely had stopped rolling when the boys began their race down the lawn toward the water.

Before they reached the water's edge, their squeals of delight turned to screams of distress. Hopping, grimacing, they grabbed their feet in pain. Hidden in the lush carpet of green, and now imbedded in their tender feet, were briarlike spurs. What a nasty trick for nature to play—to conceal impaling surprises in a setting so soft and inviting.

The boys soon forgot their pain and were splashing with joy in the water. But I couldn't resist a smile. Although we were far from the intensity of the city, the inseparable companions of pain and pleasure had followed us.

Madison Avenue marketing, heroes that have bad breath, and lush lawns that conceal spurs sometimes tempt me toward cynicism. "Nothing is ever as good as it appears to be," says Murphy's law, and it seems to carry more weight than many sermons. Not even Christianity itself is exempt from its harsh truth. Our faith clearly does not measure up to the claims of its popular promoters. Hidden behind the promise of peace is warfare; concealed amidst the assurances of hope is plaguing doubt. And in the shadow of great joy stands a cross.

Joy and sorrow, gain and loss. The beautiful and the ugly are never far apart in this world. Nor is it different for the people of the kingdom. The work of harvesting good grain is never free from the infestation of troublesome tares.

I wish it were otherwise. I wish that our diverse little inner-city congregation were as loving after the Sunday service as they are during it. I wish we could root out cliquishness, gossip, and the unfair use of power.

I wish the houses provided by God's people to poor families in our community were the source of uninterrupted joy and gratitude, and not a cause of sporadic family bickering and jealousy within the church.

I wish that addicted people whose hearts have been touched by the love of Christ could be wrapped in a permanent sheltering love that would protect them from the pain of withdrawal and future failures.

I wish, oh how I wish, that my dear friend and dedicated fellow worker had been spared from the brutal rape and beating that was concealed in the path of her obedient servanthood.

But alas the painful tares are always present among the growing fruit. The Lord of the harvest said it would be so. He instructed us to leave the damaging weeds alone, not to try to root them out. "For we might lose some of the good grain," he cautions us (Matt. 13:24–30).

So the pain remains. My work is not to eliminate the troublesome but to foster the wholesome. I don't need to be concerned about how it appears to others that there are tares in my field; the Lord of the harvest can handle his own public relations. Neither do I need herbicides that make the fruit appear bigger and the troubles benign. In the end these sweet poisons will produce more death than life.

Integrity and deceit, growth and brokenness, affection and hostility. They are the realities of life in the field where I live and work. To deny any aspect is to miss the full measure of life. The assurance of a good harvest in the fullness of time is enough to make the joys satisfying and the pain tolerable.

# SNOWFLAKES AND SUNSETS

I think God must detest sameness. At least he has gone to great lengths to avoid it. Every snowflake, every cloud, every flower is unique. He has created and continues to create an endless variety of trees, bugs, sunsets, and beasts. He has created billions of human beings, every one an original. All of nature is an infinite array of individually designed organisms interacting in harmonious praise to its Maker. And humans, created in the very image of their Maker, are given the high privilege of being cocreators with God.

I suspect that one of the results of the fall for humanity was the loss of some of our creativity. Not all of it, of course. We still are quite capable of creating symphonies and paintings and children and other beautiful things. But I think that sin brought with it sameness. Boredom. Monotony. Instead of remaining cocreators with God, we opted for making molds. We began making people in our own image, forcing them into conformity. We traded creativity for cloning. We found that we could accomplish certain ends more efficiently by eliminating faces and personalities and replacing them with numbers and uniforms. Regimentation became our method. We separated human beings into categories by tasks, color, intellect, health, age, sex, and a host of other useful classifications.

Soon bondage and drudgery choked out much of the fun of living. We became isolated from the rich, dynamic interaction in which all creation was to participate. We became so accomplished in efficiency that we didn't have time to stop and see the loveliness of snowflakes.

The city. A melting pot. Variety packed together in one place. A collage of humanity. A nightmare to economists. A fright to social engineers. A curse to many.

But the church—how does it view the city? Church growth experts see the city as a problem because its diversity makes homogeneous grouping difficult to achieve on a large scale. Denominations aren't able to replicate their traditional church models here very well. And keeping alive the old city structures is quite a drain on our resources. The city is making us realize that sameness is a failure.

Maybe, just maybe, God will use the city to remind us that all his unique individual masterpieces clustered together in high rises and housing projects and neighborhoods bear a reflection of his original design. Perhaps it will be in the city that the church will rediscover the richness of diversity interacting in hard-earned unity.

I wonder why God has selected for our place of final destiny the *City* of God!

# Afterword

# NEW WINESKINS FOR AN URBANIZING WORLD

The whole world is moving to the city. More than two billion of the peoples of the earth are now urban dwellers.

In our own nation, towns and farm communities are dwindling as the population of metropolitan areas rapidly expands. While cities become strong centers of commerce, culture, and capital, they also become catch basins for the people most at risk—the old, the poor, the sick, single-parent households, refugees, and outcasts. And unlike the manageable nine-to-five towns of our past, cities are complex, twenty-four-hour megasystems complete with hospitals and police, taxi drivers and chefs, janitors and merchants. The increasing velocity and diversity of human interaction can be numbing if not overwhelming.

The institutional church seems baffled by the changes forced upon it by urbanization. Traditional methods of "doing church" are clearly losing their effectiveness in the city. In Atlanta my own denomination has been closing down a church a year for the past fifteen years. Even the growing, homogeneous suburban churches (which the denomination is still able to plant) feel the threat as a sprawling urban tide moves steadily to engulf them. The same trend is true for all major denominations. The old wineskins seem unable to adapt to the new wine of the Spirit for our cities.

Yet in spontaneous, inconspicuous ways, the God of history is fitting together new forms for the urban church—bold, compassionate forms adapted to the schedules, cultures, and special needs of the city. As I communicate with urban visionaries around the country and throughout the world, I am discovering some common characteristics of these new wineskins. Almost all grow out of contact with poor and disenfranchised people. They are often multiethnic or multiracial. They are reinstituting early church practices of sharing food, homes, and material possessions with those in need. And there is a rediscovery of the importance of spiritual gifts which are distributed to all believers and give special significance to even the least in the body.

This movement seems to be flowing around, not so much through, the institutional church. It takes the forms of house churches, fellowships, intentional communities, church/parachurch hybrids, and other nontraditional structures. Although there is not much emphasis placed on formal seminary training (many lay people are emerging as leaders), there is a high regard for biblical integrity. The members and leaders of these groups are mostly young people who are turned off by the blandness of the institutional church, yet who are willing to make radical personal sacrifices for the sake of the gospel.

For example, in London over six hundred such churches and groups have sprung up in the last five years. Young, untrained, unorganized Christians are moving into the ghettos. They are exposing themselves to danger and hardship, sharing food and apartments, and giving their best years to live among the disenfranchised.

These ventures have caused no small stir among the religious establishment of London. Some cry "irresponsible" and "unaccountable." There is virtually no denominational support for these ministries. Yet their numbers continue to grow and their work profoundly impacts those inner-city areas of London that changed while the church stayed the same.

The world is urbanizing. The city is our opportunity to see firsthand how God is doing his creative work in our day. It is both fearful and wonderful, an invitation to death and incomparable life. And it is ours to discover.

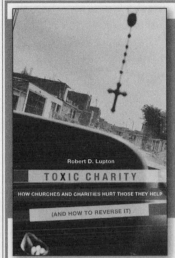

**Robert D. Lupton**

## TOXIC CHARITY

HOW CHURCHES AND CHARITIES HURT THOSE THEY HELP

(AND HOW TO REVERSE IT)

## *Why Does America Give So Much But Nothing Gets Better?*

In his newest book, TOXIC CHARITY, Robert D. Lupton exposes a growing scandal: many of our charitable efforts are actually harmful to the very people and communities we aim to help. Lupton delivers proven strategies for moving from toxic charity to transformative charity, offering a practical action plan for creating successful, empowering partnerships that are genuinely life-changing.

### Also available in ebook edition.

HarperOne
*An Imprint of* HarperCollins*Publishers*